Contents

It is estimated that the largest transfer of wealth between generations in
history will occur by the mid-twenty-first century. The most widely quoted
authority on this transfer discusses how heirs, soon to become ancestors
themselves, may become discerning souls, capable of charting a financial
and philanthropic journey tailored to their times.

The moral case for and against the 2001 repeal of the estate tax was the
missing element in the debate on this highly charged issue, Pactor argues.
Philosophical underpinnings gleaned from a half-dozen philosophers—
more so than statistics and dollar amounts—advance the case of the estate
tax as a moral imperative for a just and decent society.

A meaningful due diligence process that precedes grant making does much
more for family philanthropies than simply produce responsible grants. It
can also enhance financial stewardship, foster personal growth, and lead to
responsible behavior in all aspects of life.

Is helping our loved ones an evolutionary adaptation that is good for our
own health and well-being? This review of recent studies suggests that view
as an interpretation for altruism and hypothesizes implications for how we
care for those closest to us.

Butts asserts that where civic engagement is concerned, we need to move
beyond traditional thinking—that older people are our past and younger

people are our future—and focus on re-creating service opportunities to capture the power of young and old as volunteers and philanthropists. Service learning opportunities can embrace the "bookend generations" if they begin to use an intergenerational lens.

Cathlene Williams
Association of Fundraising Professionals

Lilya Wagner
The Center on Philanthropy at Indiana University
COEDITORS-IN-CHIEF

PHILANTHROPY ACROSS THE GENERATIONS

Dwight F. Burlingame
The Center on Philanthropy at Indiana University

EDITOR

NUMBER 42, WINTER 2003

PHILANTHROPY ACROSS THE GENERATIONS
Dwight F. Burlingame (ed.)
New Directions for Philanthropic Fundraising, No. 42, Winter 2003
Cathlene Williams, Lilya Wagner, Coeditors-in-Chief

NEW DIRECTIONS FOR PHILANTHROPIC FUNDRAISING (print ISSN 1072-172X; online
ISSN 1542-7846) is indexed in Higher Education Abstracts and Philanthropic Index.

Microfilm copies of issues and articles are available in 16 mm and 35 mm, as well as
microfiche in 105 mm, through University Microfilms Inc., 300 North Zeeb Road,
Ann Arbor, Michigan 48106-1346.

NEW DIRECTIONS FOR PHILANTHROPIC FUNDRAISING is part of the Jossey-Bass
Nonprofit and Public Management Series and is published quarterly by Wiley Sub-
scription Services, Inc., A Wiley company, at Jossey-Bass, 989 Market Street, San
Francisco, California 94103-1741.

SUBSCRIPTIONS cost $109.00 for individuals and $215.00 for institutions, agencies,
and libraries. Prices subject to change. Refer to the order form at the back of this
issue.

EDITORIAL CORRESPONDENCE should be sent to Lilya Wagner, The Center on Philanthropy at Indiana University, 550 West North Street, Suite 301, Indianapolis, IN
46202-3162, or to Cathlene Williams, Association of Fundraising Professionals,
1101 King Street, Suite 700, Alexandria, VA 22314.

www.josseybass.com

Editor's Notes

THIS ISSUE OF *New Directions for Philanthropic Fundraising* grew out of the Sixteenth Annual Symposium on Philanthropy held in Indianapolis on August 21–22, 2003. Scholars, donors, fundraisers, and other practitioners came together to discuss and reflect on issues facing donors and donees in the philanthropic relationship. The authors in this volume examine subjects ranging from the role of ethics in philanthropic agencies to challenges in giving, financial and grant-making skills, how to transform philanthropy, the importance of the estate tax, intergenerational learning and volunteering, and the health benefits of giving. The common focus is on the role of and value of philanthropy throughout the lifetime and across the generations.

Symposium participants, and this issue editor in particular, found reinforcement for the importance of giving being learned and nurtured wherever possible in our society, particularly in families. The philanthropic gift is not just a means to express social relationships. It also reinforces social bonds and provides for the actualization of reciprocity.

Paul Schervish leads the issue with a compelling and articulate statement about understanding our moral compass and how we might engage philanthropically in our communities. When individuals understand their moral biography it can help them understand how to transfer their wealth to the next generation and how to actualize their own philanthropy. The tension between supply-side and demand-side philanthropy continues to be a fruitful field for debate.

Do the wealthy have a moral duty to give back to society through the estate tax? In Chapter Two, Andrea Pactor offers a theoretical

NEW DIRECTIONS FOR PHILANTHROPIC FUNDRAISING, NO. 42, WINTER 2003 © WILEY PERIODICALS, INC.

exploration of the moral case for yes that is grounded in philosophical arguments about property and justice. Pactor argues that the wealthy have a societal responsibility to lessen the disparity between the haves and the have-nots and that this can be accomplished in part by redistribution of wealth through estate taxes. What effect the repeal of the estate tax in the United States will have on giving during life and in charitable bequests is yet to be determined.

A critical issue in the wealth transfer debate is the ability of the next generation to provide responsible financial leadership. In Chapter Three, Paul Comstock argues that the properly understood rule of investigation before investing applies as equally to one's philanthropy as to one's financial future. The due diligence process allows families to come together not only to investigate grants they wish to make but also to groom the next generation for responsible financial decision making.

Studies of giving behavior and its links to well-being suggest that there is a benefit to the giver. In Chapter Four, Stephanie Brown provides us with an understanding of recent research. The chapter suggests that *giving*, as opposed to *receiving*, is what makes for the beneficial effect in the "giving-receiving" relationship.

In Chapter Five, Donna Butts continues the theme of giving across the generations. Intergenerational service learning programs are held up as one important way to engage young and old in community service and develop the value of philanthropy in both generations.

Richard Steinberg and Mark Wilhelm in Chapter Six review current research on giving and volunteering that is being done based on the *Center on Philanthropy's Panel Study* (COPPS). COPPS provides a rich data set through which many currently unanswered questions about donors can be explored. Fundraisers will be well-served in applying this research to their practice.

How do we recognize a "philanthropic nature" in a potential donor? In Chapter Seven, James Hodge explores the techniques that fundraisers might use to identify a philanthropic inclination and shows how development professionals can work with potential donors to assist them in their life cycle of generativity. A values clarification process helps philanthropists understand their own values and explore how they might pass these values on to the next generation. "Transforming Philanthropy" is worthy of a close and reflective read.

Based on her experience working with young entrepreneurial companies to create and implement seminars in the for-profit arena, Lorna Lathram in Chapter Eight combines traditional grant-making and entrepreneurial practices to create a new approach to engaged philanthropy. If we discover our own philanthropic values, it provides the basis from which we can use philanthropy to engage in community leadership. High-performing families yield high-engagement family philanthropy.

David Smith concludes this issue with Chapter Nine, "Paved with Good Intentions." Based on his remarks for the Donikian Family Lecture on Ethics and Philanthropy, a lecture that is given annually at the Center on Philanthropy at Indiana University, Smith's chapter is informed by over thirty years of study on the role ethics plays in our lives. He provides a window through which we may view our moral journey in engaging others in philanthropic action.

Dwight F. Burlingame
Editor

DWIGHT F. BURLINGAME *is associate executive director and director of academic programs at The Center on Philanthropy, Indiana University Purdue University Indianapolis.*

The intergenerational transfer of philanthropy involves teaching and learning that enables subsequent generations, like the disciples in all spiritual traditions, to become generative bearers and propagators rather than simple receivers and distributors of the moral citizenship of financial care.

1

The inheritance of wealth and the commonwealth: The ideal of *paideia* in an age of affluence

Paul G. Schervish

THE TRANSMISSION OF PHILANTHROPY across the generations is the transfer of a spiritual agency of material capacity, care for others, and a process of conscientious decision making and choice. The intergenerational transmission of philanthropy is less a matter of shepherding heirs to become caretakers of existing philanthropic instruments and endeavors as it is a matter of guiding heirs to become agents who reconstitute for their own time and in their own way the relationship between wealth and the commonwealth. As such, the intergenerational transfer of philanthropy involves a

Note: I am grateful to the T. B. Murphy Foundation Charitable Trust and the Lilly Endowment for their support of this research. I also wish to thank my colleague John Havens for his graciousness and expertise in providing the bulk of the findings I present here, and Cheryl Stults for her generous and competent editorial assistance.

NEW DIRECTIONS FOR PHILANTHROPIC FUNDRAISING, NO. 42, WINTER 2003 © WILEY PERIODICALS, INC.

particular method of teaching and learning that enables subsequent generations, like the disciples in all spiritual traditions, to become generative bearers and propagators rather than simple receivers and distributors of the moral citizenship of financial care. Our heirs are the descendants of our philanthropic prospects and purposes. And in short course, they will become the ancestors for a subsequent generation of descendants. It is our higher purpose not to make them mirrors of ourselves but discerning souls capable of charting a financial and philanthropic trajectory tailored to their times.

In this chapter, I make a case on behalf of the next generation rather than against them—as is so often done in content and tone by those of us who are eager to make our offspring responsible according to our lights. I consider our offspring to be agents and subjects like ourselves rather than mere objects of our training whom we are attempting to get to do what we think should be done. As I have found over the course of my years of research, we and our peers approach our own philanthropy from inclination and inspiration. But when it comes to our children, we scold and cajole in order to pass on philanthropic impulses. For many reasons, many of them noble, we engage in much pushing and shoving even of our adult children, trying to get them to do what we want them to do: be philanthropic, be involved in the family foundation, do community service.

Although we resist being told our specific duties in regard to wealth—temporal and financial—and the commonwealth, we still tend to tell the next generation what their duties are. Let me be clear, my approach does not remove obligation, duty, and responsibility from our heirs in regard to wealth and the commonwealth. What it does remove is our tendency to cajole and replaces it with a more abundant, deeper, and productive approach for passing on the sense and sensibility of care to those who follow us. Instead of telling our children the specifics of their vocation of care, we do better to teach them well about how to discern their own vocation. Passing on a philanthropic orientation to the next generation is at best passing on a method for conscientious decision making. Why is this is so important? In the end, we will not be there to ensure that our heirs do what we wanted them to do, and so we need to do our best to help them be continuous finders and bearers of their duties, not just replicate ours.

In the first section of the chapter I draw on an essay by John Maynard Keynes to help us understand the material and cultural conditions of the early twenty-first century. In the second section, I summarize several elements of the material heritage we will leave our children, including a substantial transfer of wealth, and indicate the implications of these trends for the historical circumstances of wealth and philanthropy that our heirs will face. The third section examines the meaning of moral biography as the confluence of material capacity and moral compass, and how our calling today is to provide our heirs the opportunity conscientiously to shape their own moral biographies based on the distinctive characteristics of the future they will inhabit. In the fourth section, I explore two elements of how we might best go about helping our children and grandchildren form their own moral biographies. I focus especially on the communication of *paideia*, the Greek ideal of formative education and the meaning of culture, as the ideal of our teachings, and on discernment as a process of decision making aimed at clarifying philanthropic resources, purposes, and mode of implementation. In the conclusion, I exhort those of my generation to make it our vocation to help our children freely discover their own vocation.

A material and spiritual inheritance

In addition to the impending intergenerational transfer of wealth there will be a corresponding intergenerational transfer of philanthropic practice. Besides a material inheritance, we need to be concerned about a spiritual inheritance. In addition to charting the growing material capacity that our heirs will face, we need to reflect on the issues of character and character formation we want to teach our children and grandchildren.

John Maynard Keynes had something prescient to say about this spiritual inheritance in his 1929 essay "The Economic Possibilities for Our Grandchildren." According to Keynes,

The economic problem [of scarcity] may be solved, or at least within sight of solution, within a hundred years. . . . When the accumulation of wealth is no longer of high social importance, there will be great changes in the code of morals . . . [such that] the love of money as a possession—as distinguished from the love of money as a means to the enjoyments and realities of life—will be recognized for what it is, a somewhat disgusting morbidity, one of those semi-criminal, semi-pathological propensities which one hands over with a shudder to the specialists in mental disease. [1933b, pp. 366, 369]

I believe that despite the suffering wrought by recalcitrant world poverty, we, our children, and our grandchildren are in the midst of what Keynes characterized as "the greatest change which has ever occurred in the material environment of life for human beings in the aggregate" (Keynes, 1933b, p. 372). For the first time, we are arriving at the juncture when "we shall be able to rid ourselves of the many pseudo-moral principles . . . by which we have exalted some of the most distasteful of human qualities" (p. 369). In this new dispensation of material wherewithal, for the first time each human being will confront what Keynes says is "his real, his permanent problem—how to use his freedom from pressing economic cares, how to occupy the leisure which science and compound interest will have won for him, to live wisely and agreeably and well" (p. 367). In this new material dispensation we will find, says Keynes, that "the nature of one's duty to one's neighbor has changed. For it will remain reasonable to be economically purposive for others even after it has ceased to be reasonable for oneself" (p. 372).

There are in Keynes's reflections two connected topics. The first is his forecast of an unprecedented material wealth; the second is his speculation about the potential consequences of that financial advance for spiritual and cultural development. In some ways there is nothing else to speak about when addressing the intergenerational transfer of philanthropic practice than each of these two topics and their mutual relationship.

Material wherewithal

Without going into detail here, I will note and briefly comment on ten empirical findings that are relevant to the financial trends Keynes speaks about and that are relevant to the potential change in cultural orientation that Keynes says will ensue from those financial trends.

First, according to calculations by John Havens from the Federal Reserve Flow of Funds, average annual real growth in wealth from 1950 to 2001 has been at 3.34 percent, despite a dozen economic recessions over this period. The implication is that Keynes's projection of growth in wealth over the one hundred years from 1930 to 2030 is reasonable if growth simply continues at the rate of the past fifty-one years.

Second, this fifty-one-year trend in growth of wealth sheds a new light on our wealth transfer projections. We have emphasized the five-decade projection of a $41 trillion transfer, which when updated to 2002 dollars totals $45 trillion, including $7 trillion in charitable bequests. But if the average real rate of growth in wealth is the same as it has been over the past fifty-one years (that is, 3.34 percent), then we are really looking at a wealth transfer of between $80 trillion and $150 trillion with charitable bequests totaling between $13 trillion and $27 trillion (in 2002 dollars)—in addition to at least $20 trillion in inter vivos giving (Havens and Schervish, 1999; Havens and Schervish, 2003). Moreover, all this occurs without making individuals more charitably inclined, but results simply from projecting forward the charitable dispositions of the population that were in effect around 1995—before the spurt of charitable giving in the late 1990s. In a word, these projections do not take into account the intensification of charitable proclivities that all of us are hoping to generate among ourselves and our progeny.

The third point is that there already exists a strong association between greater financial capacity and greater charitable giving. Whether measured by wealth or income, the 7 percent of households at the top of the distributions ($1 million in net worth or $140,000 in annual income) contribute 50 percent of all the inter vivos yearly charitable giving. Charitable bequests are even more highly skewed toward the upper end. The .07 percent of estates valued at $20 million or more contribute 44 percent of the value of all charitable bequests while the 5.1 percent of estates valued at $5 million or more contribute 66 percent of the value of all the charitable bequests (Havens and Schervish, 2003).

As strong as the general association between finances and philanthropy may be, it is even stronger among those who identify themselves as financially secure—those who, in Keynes's terms, have "solved" the "economic problem" for themselves and their heirs. Perhaps the most important general contribution of sociology to the study of economic life is that assessment of one's personal financial status is not simply a matter of objective criteria. Individuals always define their financial resources and aspirations relative to subjective values and norms and in view of comparative assessments with their reference groups. We have found (Schervish and Havens, 2001) that at every level of income and wealth, the higher individuals rate themselves as subjectively financially secure, the greater amount they give to charity, the greater the percentage of income they contribute, and the greater the percentage of wealth they give. There are direct implications of this finding for Keynes's prognostication. One model about the relationship between wealth and care for others is that the more affluent one is, the more self-centered and uncaring one becomes. The opposite model is more akin to Keynes's view, as we have heard: the more financially secure one becomes, the more one becomes "economically purposive for others even after it has ceased to be reasonable for oneself" (Keynes, 1933b, p. 372).

After interviewing hundreds of wealth holders and analyzing surveys, I subscribe to neither of these two polar models. In my view, wealth is Janus-faced. It proffers both opportunities and obstacles to care for others. Wealth does not automatically lead individuals to be either other-directed or self-directed. What it does in every instance is expand the horizons of choice and raise the questions: "What should I choose to do with my financial resources? Given the quantitative expansion of my choices, what should the qualitative content of those choices be?" Great wealth always leads to the great question: "What could I do, should I choose to do it?" It never automatically answers this question one way or another. But as the foregoing findings on financial security and charitable giving indicate, there is some reason to believe that wealth does create an opening for philanthropy.

Our explanation of why this occurs is that at some point the very wealthy, although they are always faced with a budget constraint, no longer experience a budget constraint around their standard of living. Such individuals are financially independent and have achieved financial transcendence—meaning that their stream of resources has exceeded the stream of their expenditures for the entire foreseeable future. For those who recognize that the difference between their stream of resources and their stream of expenditures is not only positive but permanent and even growing, there is an inclination to allocate the redundant financial resources to charity. As Thomas Murphy (2001, pp. 34–35), a self-reflective philanthropist, explains:

Given the generally accepted assumption that one provides first for oneself and one's family and does so at some level of lifestyle, philanthropy enters into the decision-making process [in a more significant manner] when the difference between the expected level of income, current and future, and expected level of expense, current and future, to maintain and enhance one's standard of living is substantial and relatively permanent as measured by the subjectively determined criteria of the decision maker. . . . The extent to which this difference (discretionary income) between income and expense is positive quantifies the financial resources available for philanthropic activities. The extent to which this difference is perceived as permanent strengthens the case for allocating some of the resources for philanthropy. The extent to which the difference is positive, permanent, and growing in magnitude enhances the philanthropic allocation.

For those who have solved Keynes's economic problem for themselves and their spouses as well as for their children and grandchildren, what remains other than additional investment and business formation is philanthropy. Examining individual financial plans to discern the extent to which wealth holders actually act in the way Murphy describes and Keynes expects is part of our current research agenda. If financial security does in fact lead to increased charitable giving, the consequences are obvious for the forthcoming generations, which in all probability may be even more financially secure than their parents.

Another aspect of the material conditions undergirding the inheritance of wealth and the commonwealth is John Havens's and my new findings on the positive relationship between estate tax repeal and charitable bequests. Virtually every analysis to date on the relationship of estate tax to charitable giving confounds those two groups. David Joulfaian (2000) analyzes the effects of the estate tax on charitable bequests for a sample of estate tax filers in 1992. He concludes that "In the absence of the estate tax . . . charitable bequests may decline by about 12 percent" (p. 21). Other research indicates downturns in charitable bequests of 22 percent (Gale, Hines, and Slemrod, 2001) and between 24 and 45 percent (Clotfelter and Schmalbeck, 1996). The primary innovation in our analysis is to model the fact that the relationship between wealth, the estate tax, and charitable giving is dramatically different for estates where there is a surviving spouse (first estates) and estates where there is no surviving spouse (final estates). Although Joulfaian does not pursue this analysis, he does provide the separate statistics on the estates of married and unmarried decedents. Our analysis uses his data to conduct our separate analyses of first and final estates. These results indicate that repeal of the estate tax would not reduce charitable bequests by 12 percent but would increase total charitable bequests by 35 percent.

We are not suggesting that our preliminary findings form the basis for policy at this point. We are claiming, however, that conventional wisdom about estate tax repeal reducing charitable bequests is not as certain as it is made out to be. Also, our findings suggest that if the repeal of the estate tax were to occur, two things would happen. More dollars would flow to charity at the death of final decedents. And because more wealth would also flow to heirs, those heirs would be more likely to receive or reach financial security and at an earlier period in their lives. This would also result in more dollars going to charity in inter vivos giving and in bequests.

Finally, there is the material consideration that repeal of the estate tax may lead to greater economic growth. Although most economists who study the impact of estate tax repeal do not support repeal because of equity considerations, negative effects on wealth distribution, and a negative impact on charitable giving, they generally conclude that repeal will rationale economic activity sufficiently enough to increase economic growth. Unproductive, economic-aimed tax-avoidance and lower, distorted investment incentives all reduce economic growth. Now, those familiar with our wealth transfer model know that we model wealth transfer based on separate scenarios of real annual growth in wealth of 2 percent, 3 percent, and 4 percent. The 2 percent scenario produces a $45 trillion transfer (in 2002 dollars) with $7 trillion in charitable bequests. At 3 percent growth the transfer is $80 trillion with $13 trillion going to charity. At 4 percent real growth the figures are $150 trillion and $27 trillion (Havens and Schervish, 1999). Recalling that the real annual growth in wealth between 1950 and 2001 was 3.34 percent, it is instructive to consider what additional increments in standard of living, employment, income, and philanthropy would ensue if repeal of the estate tax nudged the growth rate in wealth above 2 percent and ideally even above the historic level of the past five decades.

The spiritual inheritance of wealth and the commonwealth: Moral biography

I now turn to the cultural or spiritual side of John Maynard Keynes's historical forecast. My interpretation of Keynes's combination of economic and cultural destiny is that he is offering an insight into the meaning of moral biography (see Schervish, Coutouskis, and Lewis, 1994; Schervish, 1994) in the first third of the twenty-first century. A moral biography is a life lived at the crossroads of material capacity and personal character, of empowerment and moral compass, of choice and wisdom. The account of Moses' biography in the Book of Exodus is an example of a life told as a moral biography. His family has left him on the banks of the Nile so that he would be able to thrive outside the harsh conditions of an enslaved family.

Moses is brought into the household of the Pharaoh and becomes the heir apparent. He exercises capacity in the name of the Pharaoh and according to the moral compass of his vice regency. But in the view of his kin, Moses, despite his capacity, actually lacks moral compass until he learns of his ancestry, abandons his empowerment, and flees to the mountains. There, he regains his moral bearing but works as a shepherd with no singular capacity. In the manifestation of the burning bush, the Lord reconstitutes Moses' moral biography, giving him a new moral compass and the worldly capacity to accomplish it. So equipped, Moses returns to the fray, going miracle for miracle with the Pharaoh, eventually breaking his resolve and demonstrating a nobler moral bearing. With moral compass turning into geographic compass, Moses leads his people through the Red Sea from the land of slavery to the land of milk and honey.

It is our goal, too, for our children and ourselves to be like Moses in the sense of finding and implementing a moral biography that links capacity and moral compass in all realms of daily life. Over the years, we have heard both wealthy and middle-class parents talk about four moral realms they wish to teach their children regarding financial capacity. One is the realm of accumulation. Parents want to make sure their children learn the value of work, gain an attitude of industriousness, and practice honest effort. The second realm is consumption. Here, parents strive to implant a non-materialistic disposition, to limit consumption, and to provide a rationale for not buying everything they can afford. The third moral bearing in which parents wish to instruct their children is social. They want their children to grow up without the elitist attitude that their financial privilege makes them better than others. Fourth, they are concerned with savings and investment. Finally, there is allocation of wealth to meet the needs of others among family and friends, and through philanthropy.

When it comes to forming a financial morality, I do not privilege the teaching and learning of allocation and philanthropy over the other four realms. Philanthropy is not necessarily a higher calling than care of family, making investments, starting a business that creates wealth and jobs, supporting one's parents, or making personal gifts to friends in need. Attention to the relationship between capacity and character in all five realms makes up a moral biography in the age of affluence. Still, as I have said earlier, in such an age of affluence, philanthropy becomes more materially possible, and under the proper circumstances, more personally engaging.

Paideia: The formative knowledge of the spiritual inheritance

What do we teach our children so that they invite in and answer the foregoing array of questions with intelligence, empathy, and action? Werner Jaeger, the renowned Harvard classics scholar, proposes the notion of *paideia* (1943–1945, 1961) as the underlying content of all efforts of teaching and learning. Paideia is simultaneously a method of schooling, what the student learns and embodies, and the cultural consciousness of a people. Although today Jaeger is criticized in some quarters for being a Hellenocentric, his understanding of paideia remains profound. According to Jaeger, paideia in the Greek tradition is essentially formative teaching and learning. It concerns the communication and internalization not just of information, but of a corresponding personal formation and community culture. Paideia is the etymological and substantive root of pedagogy, the purpose of which is to produce "a conscious ideal of education and culture" (Vol. 2, p. 5). It is the kind of teaching carried out by God. "Lo Theos paidagogei ton kosmon" ("God formatively educates the cosmos"), says Plato. Paideia is effective teaching and learning. In theological and literary language, it is sacramental and symbolic—it creates what it teaches. It begets "the wheeling around of the whole soul towards the light of the Idea of Good, the divine origin of the universe" (Vol. 2, p. 295). It generates a rich and integrated amalgamation of elements (*krasis*) rather than a simple physical mixture (*mixis*). In the end, paideia *effects* a human agent who is an active carrier of a living ideal; it is not the implanting of a static code. As such it is a breathing, working knowledge.

Paideia is both a way of choosing and deciding with wisdom, and the personal and cultural outcome of that choosing. It is a way of thinking, feeling, and acting—the trinity of human capacities that all the great theological, philosophical, and social-scientific traditions distinguish but view as three faces of an integrated practice. Eastern traditions refer to the chakras of path, oth, and kath—head, heart, and stomach—as the three "brains" that are to be forged into an integrated and balanced union. The parallel Greek virtues are the true, the beautiful, and the good; the Christian virtues are wisdom, love, and justice. Auguste Comte and Ludwig Feuerbach repeatedly speak explicitly of the human essence as revolving around thinking, feeling, and acting. And in my view, the murky and inchoate notion of praxis used by Aristotle to mean practice as opposed to gnosis or abstract knowledge, and in more recent times used most frequently, but not exclusively, in the Marxist and Frankfurt schools, can be clarified as the dialectical practice of paideia in which thinking, feeling, and acting are mutually constitutive.

In addition to paideia being the trinity of practice that creates for the soul a humanism, as opposed to an individualism, paideia is also the trinity of thinking, feeling, and acting that forms the practices of home and culture. Just as paideia plays out in the microcosm of the individual heart, it also plays out in the mesocosm of home, and in the macrocosm of community and culture. It is the basis for what I call "the moral citizenship of care" (Schervish and Havens, 2002; Schervish, in press). These are patterns of thinking, feeling, and acting that constitute those realms of personal and social life as a free and voluntary social relationship of care. Commerce and politics are at their best embodiments of paideia, but generally function under the sway of markets. There, individuals attend to needs mainly because the needs are signaled by a medium of dollars or votes that are necessary for the material survival of commercial and political agents. This is known in economics as responding to *effective demand*. It is *effective* because the suppliers are "caused" to meet a demand for the sake of their own survival. In civil society, which is the realm of philanthropy, needs of others are met to the extent individuals are sensitized to them and to their priority by virtue of being imbued with character-forming paideia. This I call responding to *affective demand*. It is *affective* because the suppliers of resources to meet needs choose to provide resources to the extent they are sensitized to do so on the basis of some empathetic connection to those in need.

Discernment: How paideia is taught and learned

As our children enter "the greatest change which has ever occurred in the material environment of life for human beings in the aggregate" (Keynes, 1933b, p. 372), something new will occur. "The nature of one's duty to one's neighbour is changed," says Keynes, and we become "economically purposive for others" (p. 372). How do we engage our children in fathoming "the nature of one's duty to one's neighbour," and specifically in regard to the prospects of philanthropy for their own era? It is not by getting them to do what we do or by imposing on them foreign obligations. Rather, the future of philanthropy will thrive to the extent that we educate our children to shape their own philanthropic vocation—that is, teach them a method of discernment by which they will freely make wise financial decisions not only in regard to themselves but in regard to others as well. In other words, the question is not how to communicate our directions to our heirs when we are present, but how to help them set their own directions when we are absent.

The process of discernment, which I consider to be the key to teaching and learning economic paideia, is a method of decision making by which individuals are helped to uncover for themselves, rather than be told, the prospects and purposes of their material capacity in the context of the prospects and purposes of their spiritual compass. The outcome of a discernment process is a spiritually attuned allocation of financial resources in which the needs of self, family, and world are attended to simultaneously. Clearly, when heirs are young, discernment is less self-directed than when they become more capable and responsible for their own decisions. But from the time our progeny are old enough to make free decisions, our best aspiration ought be to convert them from the execution of the moral biography we set for them to the moral biography they chart for themselves. Communicating how to make decisions in regard to financial production, consumption, disposition, and allocation is the key to ensuring that our children will make wise decisions about linking capacity and moral compass when we are no longer commanding their obedience, and when they are living in circumstances that will be uniquely their own and their era's.

Discernment is derived from Latin, "to sift apart." It is a process of gaining clarity, insight, perception, or sagacity by means of self-reflection in an environment of liberty and inspiration. When understood and carried out as connected to the ultimate goal of life, both financial practices *and* the decision-making process guiding them are not just moral but *spiritual practices*. Carrying out practices in the light of one's ultimate goal is not something foreign or alien to people. It can be described simply as happiness, in the Aristotelian sense; the realization of social-psychological effectiveness and significance in Maslow's terms; the unity of love of God, love of neighbor, and love of self, as Thomas Aquinas puts it; or being united to the soul to Christ, as Luther says.

When applied to philanthropy, just as when applied to every other sphere, discernment is the preferred path to moral biography. In the realm of philanthropy, discernment clarifies the capacity of *charitable resources*, the moral compass of *charitable aspirations*, and how capacity and compass come together in *discerned or biographically or spiritually based charitable giving*. The *discernment of capacity* concerns the process of clarifying and implementing decisions in regard to allocating material resources to charity. The *discernment of aspirations* refers to the process of clarifying and implementing decisions in regard to determining the donor's financial purposes and charitable care. The *discernment of choice* concerns the process of clarifying and implementing decisions about how to combine material capacity and moral aspiration in ways that are personally formative for the individual, while at the same time meeting the needs of others.

In the end, discernment results in conscientious answers to the following six crucial questions, which can be viewed as the curriculum of paideia generating the spiritual inheritance for culture, home, and heart.

Is there anything you want to do?

That is important to do as an act of care for others?

With what type and amount of resources?

According to what timetable?

That you can do better through philanthropy than through government or commerce?

And that enables you to identify with the fate of others, express gratitude for blessings, and achieve deeper personal happiness—that is, effectiveness and significance—for yourself and others at the same time?

The main implication of discernment for passing along the spiritual inheritance of philanthropic paideia is that when individuals are granted the opportunity to reflect on their material capacities and spiritual inclinations in an atmosphere where charitable duty is self-discovered, it is more wholeheartedly pursued and sustained. Philanthropy is taken up with fuller hearts and deeper pockets.

Bearers of paideia

For Jaeger, as we have seen, paideia is "the wheeling around of the whole soul" into a self-chosen direction of transformation (1943–1945, Vol. 2, p. 295). Our children are going to have to live in a world with wealth we never dreamt about and in circumstances we cannot predict. And so they will need to be not just hearers but bearers of paideia. A few years ago, I was asked by a reporter writing an article on Christmas giving to explain why the Salvation Army is so successful in its fundraising and in carrying out its work. The answer that came to me, I still consider correct. It was that each member of the Salvation Army is a minister and not just a messenger. They do not simply carry out a direction set by others or pass along a message. Rather, as ministers, they are generative bearers of the purposes at the heart of their lives. This is the gift we can give our children and, indeed, the next generation as a whole—to be generative bearers of paideia, not just receivers but discoverers of their duties in their times. A new era is upon us, one in which capacity is going to be dramatically increased and for which we will need new meanings and methods for instilling moral compass in our progeny. Primary among these new meanings is paideia; primary among these new methods is discernment.

My final point is to make a case for the relatively optimistic assessment we hear from Keynes that I have consciously woven through my comments. Is it indeed possible that conscientious discernment will be taken up and implemented freely, and that there will emerge "a new code of morals" whereby our financial concern more immediately extends to our neighbor? Is there a realistic hope that we, our children, and our grandchildren will be inclined to discern our moral biographies and will not resist it? Will paideia, once tasted, incline us to seek an ever-richer food? I cannot say for sure because inclinations are based on sentiments, and sentiments are caring and uncaring. Still, in the end, I suggest that when it comes to the regions of life with liberty and inspiration, there is an affinity between the deeper desires of the soul and the prospects and purposes of philanthropy. This also applies to the author of the Book of Deuteronomy, who counsels that set before you is "life and death, blessing and curse" and that you should "choose life, that you and your descendants may live" (Deut. 30:19). This commandment, he assures, "is not too hard for you, neither is it far off. It is not in heaven, that you should say, 'Who will go up for us to heaven, and bring it to us, that we may hear it and do it?' Neither is it beyond the sea, that you should say, 'Who will go over the sea for us, and bring it to us, that we may hear it and do it?' But the word is very near you; it is in your mouth and in your heart, so that you can do it" (Deut. 30:11–14).

Let us not make it far off for our children. It is not for us to go up to heaven or beyond the sea and bring it to them. But do let us help them find how it is already in their mouths and in their hearts, so that they can do it. Let them be attracted to and rewarded by the formative paideia that is cause and consequence of their making decisions in their time and place, with their skills and vocations, to chart their own way through the verdant yet precarious forest of great affluence that they will traverse in the early twenty-first century.

Conclusion

Communicating moral compass to accompany and command the material capacity with which we will endow the next generation is my definition of offering a spiritual inheritance. Most of us think that this spiritual inheritance means in large part passing on a caring tradition to our heirs, including some disposition toward, if not actual participation in, philanthropic instruments and endeavors. We wish our children to have a philanthropic moral biography. But we sometimes succumb to the temptation to tell them the purposes and procedures of their philanthropy. Instead of giving them a moral biography, we need to help them develop one. We need to offer our children what we cherish for ourselves: the ability to make conscientious decisions about how they will use their capacity in the service of care.

Although a moral biography of financial care has always been part of an ascetic way of life, it is an especially valuable element of spiritual life in our age of affluence. As personal and social wealth expand the horizon of choice for our heirs—Keynes's grandchildren—it becomes increasingly important that we guide our heirs in developing a positive spirituality for affluent living and making wise choices among the obstacles and opportunities of affluence. For me, the key personal and cultural question of the twenty-first century for an increasing segment of the world's population is "How do I fashion my own, my children's, and my community's spiritual life in an age of affluence? How will the vast growth in the quantity of choice be translated into a deeper development in the quality of choice?"

To answer these questions requires an urgency about, and method for, clarifying the level of our financial capacity and how best to allocate it with moral compass. This, I believe, will increasingly include conscientious decisions about financial care in the form of charitable giving. This is best done within a broader moral biography of financial care that deals with accumulation, consumption, disposition, and allocation, including the giving and receiving of a material and spiritual inheritance. In order to animate such a spiritual inheritance for the next generation, the greatest gift by us to those that follow is that of paideia. Teaching and learning paideia is not automatic, but neither is it alien. The conscientious self-formation of discerned decision making in the light of one's ultimate end is the path to happiness for me, my children, and my neighbor. We do not need to admonish so much as invite our offspring to put behind them the spiritual confinements of the *"economic problem"* and assume the prayers, works, joys, and sufferings of *"the permanent problem of the human race"* (Keynes, 1933b, p. 366, italics in original), namely, "to reap the spiritual fruits from our material conquests" (Keynes, 1933a, p. 354).

Let us teach our children well the responsibilities of their capacities but in a way that enables them to find their own array of aspirations and agendas. We do better to help our progeny find and respond to their own burning bush than route them to ours. For it is not just paideia, but self-paideia that we want them to develop. As Werner Jaeger writes: the Greeks "were the first to [formulate the notion] that education means deliberately molding human character in accordance with an ideal" (1943–1945, Vol. 1, p. xxii). "Education is the process by which a community preserves and transmits its physical and intellectual character" (Vol. 1, p. xiii). And Jaeger adds, "Other nations made gods, kings, spirits: the Greeks

alone made men." Let us make discerning progeny. In the conclud-
ing paragraph of his book *Early Christianity and Greek Paideia*, Jaeger
(1961) writes that by bringing the notion of paideia up to its usage in
the fourth century, "it is evident that what we have been dealing
with in this study is not only the last chapter in the history of the
ideal of paideia in the late ancient Greek world but also the prologue
to the history of its medieval Latin transformations" (p. 101). What
I have been dealing with here is not only the last chapter in the history of the ideal of paideia in an age of scarcity but also the prologue
to the history of paideia in an age of affluence.

References

Clotfelter, C. T., and Schmalbeck, R. L. "The Impact of Fundamental Tax
Reform on Nonprofit Organizations." In H. J. Aaron and W. G. Gale (eds.),
Economic Effects of Fundamental Tax Reform (211–246). Washington, D.C.:
Brookings Institution Press, 1996.

Gale, W. G., Hines J. R. Jr., and Slemrod, J. (eds.) *Rethinking Estate and Gift
Taxation*. Washington, D.C.: Brookings Institution Press, 2001.

Havens, J. J., and Schervish, P. G. *Millionaires and the Millennium: New Esti-
mates of the Forthcoming Wealth Transfer and the Prospects for a Golden Age of
Philanthropy*. Boston: Social Welfare Research Institute, Boston College,
Oct. 1999. [www.bc.edu/research/swri].

Havens, J. J., and Schervish, P. G. "Why the $41 Trillion Wealth Transfer
Estimate Is Still Valid: A Review of Challenges and Questions." Journal of
Gift Planning, Jan. 2003, 7 (1), 11–14, 47–50.

Jaeger, W. *Paideia: The Ideals of Greek Culture* (Vols. 1–3). (G. Highet, trans.).
New York: Oxford University Press, 1943–1945.

Jaeger, W. *Early Christianity and Greek Paideia*. Cambridge, Mass.: Harvard
University Press, 1961.

Joulfaian, D. "Estate Taxes and Charitable Bequests by the Wealthy" (NBER
Working Paper 7663). Washington, D.C.: Office of Tax Analysis, U.S.
Department of the Treasury, 2000.

Keynes, J. M. "Clissold." In J. M. Keynes (ed.), *Essays in Persuasion* (pp.
349–357). London: Macmillan, 1933a. (Originally published 1927)

Keynes, J. M. "Economic Possibilities for Our Grandchildren." In J. M.
Keynes (ed.), *Essays in Persuasion* (pp. 358–373). London: Macmillan, 1933b.
(Originally published 1930)

Luther, M. "Concerning Christian Liberty." In C. W. Eliot (ed.), *The Harvard Classics* (Vol. 36; pp. 353–397). New York: Collier, 1910.

Murphy, T. B. "Financial and Psychological Determinants of Donors' Capacity to Give." In E. R. Tempel and D. F. Burlingame (eds.), *Understanding
the Needs of Donors: The Supply Side of Charitable Giving*. New Directions in
Philanthropic Fundraising, no. 28. San Francisco: Jossey-Bass, 2001.

Schervish, P. G. "The Moral Biographies of the Wealthy and the Cultural Scripture of Wealth." In P. G. Schervish (ed.), *Wealth in Western Thought: The Case for and Against Riches.* Westport, Conn.: Praeger, 1994.

Schervish, P. G. "The Sense and Sensibility of Philanthropy and the Moral Citizenship of Care." In D. H. Smith (ed.), *Paved with Good Intentions.* Bloomington: Indiana University Press, in press.

Schervish, P. G., Coutouskis, P. E., and Lewis, E. *Gospels of Wealth: How the Rich Portray Their Lives.* Westport, Conn.: Praeger, 1994.

Schervish, P. G., and Havens, J. J. "The Mind of the Millionaire: Findings from a National Survey on Wealth with Responsibility." In E. R. Tempel (ed.), *Understanding Donor Dynamics: The Organizational Side of Charitable Giving.* New Directions in Philanthropic Fundraising, no. 32. San Francisco: Jossey-Bass, 2001.

Schervish, P. G., and Havens, J. J. "The Boston Area Diary Study and the Moral Citizenship of Care." *Voluntas: International Journal of Nonprofit and Voluntary Organizations,* 2002, *13* (1), 47–71.

PAUL G. SCHERVISH *is professor of sociology and director of the Social Welfare Research Institute at Boston College, and National Research Fellow at the Indiana University Center on Philanthropy.*

*A historical review of philosophers who have con-
sidered the role of the wealthy in society is presented
and the moral implications of this controversial tax
discussed.*

2

The moral case for the estate tax

Andrea K. Pactor

THE CONTROVERSIAL DEBATE over the repeal of the estate tax in
recent years makes little sense when one considers how few people
are affected by the tax and the relatively insignificant amount of
federal revenue collected through it. The debate only occasionally
addresses the broader implications of the estate tax on public policy,
tax policy, the relationship between the extremely wealthy and society, the role of the government in effecting redistribution of wealth,
and the social and moral consequences on charitable organizations.
It takes on deeper meaning, however, when grounded in an analysis of the relationships between the wealthy and social responsibility and between justice and charity.

Although the estate tax was introduced in 1916 to help finance
World War I, its continuing presence raises important moral questions. What does it mean to flourish humanely? How should our
society be structured? How does one balance the interests of individuals with the interests of society? What are our moral obligations to one another? This chapter suggests that estate tax
advocates will strengthen their case by careful examination of philosophical theories about property and justice. A brief description of
the estate tax and the population that is affected by it is followed

NEW DIRECTIONS FOR PHILANTHROPIC FUNDRAISING, NO. 42, WINTER 2003 © WILEY PERIODICALS, INC.

by a summary of the arguments for and against the tax. In the second section, a historical review of philosophical theories on property and justice provides substance for advancing the moral case for this tax. The final section considers the moral implications of the estate tax on philanthropy.

Historical background

In May 2001 Congress passed the Economic Growth and Tax Relief Reconciliation Act of 2001, which radically changed federal tax law for estate taxes. Guidelines for the estate tax allow the head of a household to transfer an unlimited amount of assets to the surviving spouse. A certain amount of property and other assets are exempt from the federal estate tax. To avoid immediate revenue loss, the 2001 act raised the exemption gradually from $675,000 in 2001 to $3.5 million in 2009 while at the same time lowering the tax rate from 55 percent in 2001 to 45 percent in 2009. After an unlimited exemption and a zero tax rate in 2010, exemptions return in 2011 to the 2001 level. There are efforts to make the repeal permanent.

Considering the estate tax's nearly eighty-year history, Gale and Slemrod (2003) suggested five reasons why the debate about it intensified in recent years: the stock market boom, an aging population, the budget surplus, and intensive lobbying. . . . Also, the estate tax raises controversial issues.

It is difficult to understand the furor over the estate tax when the numbers alone are examined. Only America's most wealthy citizens feel the tax's impact. The estate tax affects less than 2 percent of the population. When the exemption rises to $3.5 million in 2009, even fewer individuals will be affected. In 1997, twenty-four estates paid nearly half of all estate taxes. In fiscal year 2001 the federal government collected $29.2 billion in estate and gift taxes, representing only 1.4 percent of the total federal tax revenue.

When the cost of the repeal is calculated, the issue assumes larger significance. The Center on Budget and Policy Priorities estimates the cost of the repeal at $294 billion during the 2002 to 2011 period and three-fourths of a trillion dollars for the 2012 to 2021 period (Lay and Friedman, 2003). Those figures do not include the corresponding revenue loss at the state level. The center states that the full financial impact of the repeal will be felt when the baby boom generation retires in large numbers, placing heavy burdens on Social Security, Medicare, and Medicaid programs. In addition, it will reduce funds for "other priority needs such as improving educational opportunities, expanding health insurance coverage, and reducing child poverty. It also would leave fewer funds for tax cuts targeted to average working families" (Lay and Friedman, 2003).

The impact of the loss of the estate tax on charitable giving is difficult to assess in finite terms because there is no firm evidence on the extent to which tax incentives motivate giving. Giving by bequest has represented less than 10 percent of all charitable giving over the last thirty years, but the dollars may be difficult to replace, especially in a weak economy. Between 1970 and 2000 giving by bequest ranged from a low of $5.29 billion, or 5.2 percent of total giving, in 1979, to a high of $16.02 billion, or 7.9 percent of total giving, in 2000, in inflation-adjusted dollars (*Giving USA 2001*, 2002). The Council for Advancement and Support of Education (CASE) reported that educational institutions receive about $3 billion from bequests annually (Council for the Advancement and Support of Education, 2003). CASE acknowledged that although "it is difficult to say precisely how much those institutions would lose as a result of appeal, estate tax considerations do figure significantly into the decisions of many major donors."

The philanthropic community is divided over the impact of the repeal of the estate tax on charitable giving. Two vocal experts have expressed their opinions in the pages of the *Chronicle of Philanthropy.* Paul Schervish argued in January 2001 that "repealing [the estate tax] would lead to greater national and personal economic growth, encourage charitable giving to be more of a voluntary act than one spurred by tax incentives, and mobilize for charity the increasing affluence and philanthropic inclinations of many Americans" (n.p.). Schervish cited data from two studies that revealed (1) a shift in giving from heirs to charity and (2) a 15 percent increase in allocation of assets to charity between 1992 and 1997. He also predicted that the estate tax repeal would produce more income and more jobs, thus enabling more Americans to be charitable.

William H. Gates, Sr., and Chuck Collins presented an opposing view in a January 2003 article. They concluded that the "combined 18 percent decline in resources going to the civic and public sphere makes a pretty good case for not encouraging the super-wealthy to dictate tax policy" (p. 49). The authors cited data from three studies that indicate that the estate tax repeal will negatively affect charitable giving. The study sponsored by INDEPENDENT SECTOR and Council on Foundations anticipated a reduction in charitable bequests of $3 billion in 1996 and $7.3 billion in 2001. A U.S. Treasury study predicted a decline of some $5 to $6 billion in charitable giving in 1999. David Joulfaian estimated a 13 to 31 percent decline in charitable giving, depending on the variables (Gates and Collins, 2003). His conclusion that "the higher the tax rate, the greater the giving" is supported by this sentiment, expressed in a popular business magazine. "People gain satisfaction from charitable giving. It makes them feel good, and they tend to consume more of this feeling as their incomes rise" (Seligman, 1998, p. 95).

Most vocal about the impact of the estate tax repeal have been economists, tax analysts, lawyers, researchers, and a few philanthropic leaders. Statistics, numbers, and dollar amounts have crowded the conversation. But the status of the estate tax is more than a partisan political issue. Too few spokespeople have referred to the broader moral and social implications of the highly charged issue. Examination of the philosophical underpinnings of this issue suggests a fairly clear rationale for maintaining the estate tax with minor alterations.

Philosophers' positions

Framed in a moral context, the debate about the estate tax has implications for the relationship of the wealthy to society. For centuries philosophers have tried to determine how society should be structured. They have wrestled with how one balances the interests of the individual with the interests of society. Philosophers such as Hugo Grotius, John Locke, Immanuel Kant, and John Stuart Mill deliberated whether property ownership engenders social responsibilities. Contemporary philosophers John Rawls and Allen Buchanan add substance, clarity, and value to the debate.

Dutch philosopher Hugo Grotius (1583 to 1645) described the origins of private property as a two-step process. First God "conferred upon the human race a general right over things of a lower nature." Then, as society became more industrialized, goods were no longer divided fairly. As a result, agreements were made about who owned what. In his model, property became a "perfect" right, meaning the quality is fully present. Perfect rights imply "absolute mastery over what is [one's] own." (Schneewind, 1996, p. 58). For Grotius, the purpose of society is to safeguard each individual's possessions. Thus, property or wealth belongs to the owner. The owner has no social responsibility. Advocates of permanent repeal of the estate tax would benefit from a careful reading of Grotius's views on property because his theory provides a moral rationale for their case.

In contrast, British philosopher John Locke (1632 to 1704) argued in favor of property bringing social responsibilities, particularly in relation to the needs of the poor in an agrarian society. He said "so charity gives every Man a Title to so much out of another's plenty, as will keep him from extreme want" (Schneewind, 1996, p. 62). Locke was sensitive to economic concerns and the religious imperative to take care of the poor. By stressing that such aid was to keep individuals from "extreme want," however, Locke limited the degree of responsibility the wealthy have to the poor.

The philosophy of the German Immanuel Kant (1724 to 1804) presents a thorough and compelling argument in favor of the social responsibility of the wealthy. To Kant "justification of the institution of property rests . . . not on its own usefulness, but on its direct relation to our being moral agents." In proposing that "the sovereign within a properly constituted state has the right to use public money for the support of the indigent, and of abandoned children or children who would otherwise be left to die," Kant advocated that support for these efforts come from taxation. It was a "matter of the right of the state" that taxes from the wealthy support charitable causes (Schneewind, 1996, p. 66). In this context, Kant's categorical imperative to "act as if the maxim of thy action were to become by thy will a universal law of nature" strengthens the argument of those in favor of maintaining the estate tax (Kant, 2001, p. 174).

The utilitarianism of British John Stuart Mill (1806 to 1873) makes another claim for the social responsibility of the wealthy. Mill's Greatest Happiness Principle, a primary component of utilitarianism, obliges one to do what maximizes the total welfare of all sentient beings. In this calculation, the happiness of any one person is to count for no more or less than the happiness of any other. Mill stated that utilitarianism "could only attain its end by the general cultivation of nobleness of character, even if each individual were only benefited by the nobleness of others, and his own, so far as happiness is concerned, were a sheer deduction from the benefit" (Mill, 2001, p. 125). Mill's interpretation of the Golden Rule— "to do as you would be done by, and to love your neighbor as yourself, constitute the ideal perfection of utilitarian morality" (p. 126)—is relevant to the estate tax discussion, especially in light of John Rawls's theory.

In the second half of the twentieth century two philosophers, John Rawls and Allen Buchanan, wrote widely on issues of justice, charity, and the social responsibility of the wealthy. Rawls directly addressed the estate tax in his writings and Buchanan has done so by inference. Both present compelling reasons for maintaining the estate tax.

American John Rawls (1921 to 2002) addressed the problem of "how human beings whose interests and values put them into potential conflict can inhabit with decency a common world" (Nagel, 1999, p. 36). In 1958, Rawls, considered by some to be the most important philosopher of the twentieth century, published an essay titled "Justice and Fairness," in which he postulated two basic principles of justice. These principles support the redistribution of wealth as a way to balance inequalities in society.

First, each person participating in a practice, or affected by it, has an equal right to the most extensive liberty compatible with a like liberty for all.

Second, inequalities are arbitrary unless it is reasonable to expect that they will work out for everyone's advantage, and provided the positions and offices to which they attach, or from which they are gained, are open to all. [Nagel, 1999, p. 38]

Rawls was concerned with improving the situation of the least fortunate and as such opted "for a radically egalitarian standard of social justice" (Nagel, 1999, p. 38). Accordingly, Rawls favored the estate tax "not to raise revenue . . . but gradually and continually to correct the distribution of wealth and to prevent concentrations of power detrimental to the fair value of political liberty and fair equality of opportunity" (McCaffery, 1994, p. 281). His principles of justice and fairness were reminiscent of John Stuart Mill's Golden Rule. Rawls postulated that an individual's position in society is arbitrary and a result of luck. His theory of the Original Position asks "what self-interested people would agree to as the standard for evaluation of the basic structure of society, if they knew nothing about where they would end up in the social order" (Nagel, 1999, p. 39). Thoughtful analysis of Rawls's theory will advance the moral case for the estate tax.

American Allen Buchanan (contemporary) has examined issues of justice and charity and concluded that the realm of justice includes positive general rights. To this Duke University philosopher, the welfare state has to "provide assurance that the burden of aiding those in need is distributed fairly among the better off." Historically, the realm of justice consisted of negative rights. Buchanan expanded the realm of justice to include positive general rights by referring to the rise of social institutions such as the welfare state, which "allow the 'perfecting' of imperfect duties to aid those in need" (Buchanan, 1996, p. 102).

Buchanan sees two ways by which individuals can support such social institutions: when the contribution does not harm "one's own interests or one's other legitimate commitments and obligations," and "when one knows that others in like circumstances will contribute also" (Buchanan, 1996, p. 102). The contemporary American philosopher sees the boundary between justice and charity as "an artifact of our moral will" (p. 103). Thus, each group has the ability to construct a society that reflects its moral disposition. The theories of Rawls and Buchanan strengthen the case for the estate tax as a moral imperative for a just and decent society.

Impact on philanthropy

The moral issues surrounding the estate tax are discernable in the impact of the repeal on philanthropy. The nonprofit sector depends on a mix of giving to support, sustain, and strengthen it. Giving by bequest may represent less than 10 percent of all giving each year, but those bequests are generally large and would be difficult to replace by other types of giving. In principle, the concept of redistribution of wealth to benefit society as suggested by Locke, Kant, Mill, Rawls, and Buchanan offers strong support for the estate tax. As Rooney and Tempel emphasize, the role of the estate tax in encouraging private philanthropy is pivotal. They suggest that it "may be possible that while little wealth is being redistributed by the government, wealth is being redistributed through giving to charitable causes as a result of the existence of the estate tax and the incentive to give to charity to avoid paying the tax" (2000, p. 10).

The theories of the nineteenth- and twentieth-century philosophers imply that redistribution of wealth through taxation is appropriate to aid the needy. Mark Rosenman, a philanthropy expert, stated that "there are times when principled positions need to be taken. The function of the nonprofit sector is to be sure that basic needs are met. An action which needlessly accelerates the rich getting richer while the poor are getting poorer needs to be opposed" (Billitteri, 2000, p. 17). It is virtually impossible to find advocates who argue in print for a moral rationale for the estate tax. Rosenman also said that "at a time of growing disparity in the distribution of wealth, to cut taxes rather than increase investments in dealing with public problems is wrong-minded public policy and works against the interests that nonprofits and philanthropy ostensibly serve" (Billitteri, 2000, p. 18).

One difficulty in using the moral argument is that very few bequests directly benefit the poor. Gates and Collins (2003) cite IRS data on the distribution of bequests. More than two-thirds of the dollar amount of bequests goes to scientific, medical, educational, and religious institutions. Much goes into the creation of private foundations. Gates and Collins argue that virtually every subsector will be affected directly or indirectly by the anticipated revenue loss. Certainly, one might argue that bequests indirectly benefit all of society—rich, middle class, and poor—through support of research to cure disease, education to open the doors of opportunity, and faith-based programs to help the needy.

For example, how would the 98 percent of Americans who do not pay the estate tax respond to an appeal to maintain it based on the following case? The mission of the Massachusetts Institute of Technology, one of the leading private research universities in the country, is to advance knowledge and educate students in science, technology, and other areas of scholarship that will best serve the nation and the world in the twenty-first century. In fiscal year 2000 MIT received $29 million in bequests, approximately 14 percent of the $208.5 million it received in private support and 1.4 percent of its total income of $2 billion. With an endowment of $6.2 billion as of June 30, 2001, MIT ranked eighth among leading universities in total endowment (Billitteri, 2000; MIT Web site [www.mit.edu/giving/why/why/endowment]). The significance of bequests to an institution that is "moving to solve the mysteries of the human brain, address the environmental crisis, develop tiny technologies, and engineer better human health" cannot be underestimated (see www.mit.edu/giving/index.html). Even though bequests to MIT do not directly benefit the poor, they surely benefit society. It seems likely that the 98 percent who do not pay estate taxes would encourage those who can give to give generously. If a tax incentive motivates such substantial giving, then rich and poor alike should support it because in the end, as John Stuart Mill argued, the total welfare of all is enhanced.

Timing is everything and especially so in relation to revisions in the tax code. A Democratic president vetoed congressional action to abolish the estate tax in 1999 and 2000. A Republican president approved the repeal of the estate tax in 2001—with an eye to permanent repeal. Assuming that Gale and Slemrod (2003) are correct in their reasoning on why debate about the estate tax has intensified in the past several years, then everyone who has advocated for repeal needs to consider the changed economic landscape. As of fall 2003 the federal surplus has evaporated, the states are in dire financial straits, the economy has faltered, human service programs have been slashed, and the cost of the war in Iraq is staggering. Practical reasons to maintain the estate tax with some revision seem overwhelming.

A more compelling argument for the estate tax than can be made by all the numbers, statistics, and emotion may be based on how America perceives itself at home and around the globalized world. America is experiencing increased disparity between the haves and the have-nots. Are we a society that condones the rich getting richer and the poor getting poorer? Is it not in the self-interest of the fortunate to help the less fortunate, if only to prevent uprisings or revolution? If, as Buchanan argues, Americans have the ability to construct a society that reflects our moral disposition, then the estate tax is an exercise that encourages democracy and discourages plutocracy. There is great excitement about the anticipated intergenerational transfer of wealth in the next twenty years. Now seems an ideal time for America to reinforce the concept that the wealthiest among us, all 2 percent of them, honor their moral obligation to society—before it is too late to prevent a social crisis.

References

Billitteri, T. J. "A Taxing Dilemma: Charity Leaders Are Split on How the Estate Tax Repeal Would Affect Gifts—and Whether to Take a Stand." *Chronicle of Philanthropy*, July 27, 2000, pp. 17–18.

Buchanan, A. "Charity, Justice, and the Idea of Moral Progress." In J. B. Schneewind (ed.), *Giving: Western Ideas of Philanthropy* (pp. 98–116). Bloomington: Indiana University Press, 1996.

Council for the Advancement and Support of Education (CASE). *Position on Proposed Federal Estate Tax Repeal*. Washington, D.C.: CASE, Jan. 7, 2003. [www.case.org/govtrelations/taxpolicy/estatetax_q&a.cfm].

Gale, W. E., and Slemrod, J. "Rethinking the Estate Tax." Washington, D.C.: Brookings Institute, Mar. 12, 2003. [http://www.brook.edu/comm/confer-encereport/cr05.htm].

Gates, W. H., Sr., and Collins, C. "The New Congress Should Keep the Estate Tax." *Chronicle of Philanthropy*, Jan. 9, 2003, p. 49. [www.philan-thropy.com/premium/articles/v15/i06/06004901.htm].

Giving USA 2001. Indianapolis: American Association of Fundraising Council (AAFRC) Trust for Philanthropy, 2002.

Kant, I. "Good Will, Duty, and the Categorical Imperative." In C. Sommers and F. Sommers (eds.), *Vice and Virtue in Everyday Life* (5th ed.; pp. 167–181). Fort Worth, Tex.: Harcourt College Publishers, 2001.

Lay, I. J., and Friedman, J. *Estate Tax Repeal: A Costly Windfall for the Wealth-iest Americans.* Washington, D.C.: Center on Budget and Policy Priorities, Jan. 7, 2003. [www.cbpp.org/5–25–00tax.htm].

McCaffery, E. J. "The Political Liberal Case Against the Estate Tax." *Philos-ophy and Public Affairs*, Autumn 1994, *23*, 281–312.

Mill, J. S. "Utilitarianism." In C. Sommers and F. Sommers (eds.), *Vice and Virtue in Everyday Life* (5th ed.; pp. 120–127). Fort Worth, Tex.: Harcourt College Publishers, 2001.

Nagel, T. "Justice, Justice Shalt Thou Pursue." *The New Republic*, Oct. 25, 1999, pp. 36–41.

Rooney, P. M., and Tempel, E. R. *Repeal of the Estate Tax: Its Impact on Phi-lanthropy.* Indianapolis: Center on Philanthropy at Indiana University, Nov. 1, 2000.

Schervish, P. G. "Philanthropy Can Survive Without Estate Tax." *Chronicle of Philanthropy*, Jan. 11, 2001. [www.philanthropy.com/premium/articles/v13/i06/06004701.htm].

Schneewind, J. B. "Philosophical Ideas of Charity: Some Historical Reflec-tions." In J. B. Schneewind (ed.), *Giving: Western Ideas of Philanthropy* (pp. 54–75). Bloomington: Indiana University Press, 1996.

Seligman, D. "Is Philanthropy Irrational?" *Forbes*, June 1, 1998, pp. 94–96.

ANDREA K. PACTOR *is director of development at the Jewish Community Center Association of Indianapolis.*

Making a responsible grant requires a thoughtful and well-articulated statement of intent and an implementation process that is developed and followed by the family members. The emphasis should be on fulfilling agreed-upon objectives in the most effective, efficient, and consensual way, and the process should encourage the emergence of future leadership.

3

Responsible grant making

Paul L. Comstock

AFTER YEARS OF working in the financial services industry, I have seen that the source of most errors when completing financial transactions is insufficient information gathered prior to decision making. Obtaining the necessary information to make a good financial decision can be difficult, tedious, and to an individual without proper training, overwhelming.

Caveat emptor—"Let the buyer beware"—remains as applicable a phrase today as ever. Although most financial transactions require proper disclosure of the issues involved, knowing what to look for in that disclosure and beyond is a task that few new investors are prepared for.

Yet, for individuals who find themselves thrust into making a financial decision, having prior experience in conducting a proper inquiry is essential. This process of gathering information, or investigating before investing, is called *due diligence*. All people

NEW DIRECTIONS FOR PHILANTHROPIC FUNDRAISING, NO. 42, WINTER 2003 © WILEY PERIODICALS, INC.

serving in a financial capital oversight role, whether for the benefit of others or for their own benefit, must understand due diligence fully. It is essential to long-term responsible management of that investment as well as to the achievement of meaningful desired outcomes.

Grant making is a financial transaction. Being a responsible grant maker requires a multidimensional decision-making effort. Basically, making a grant involves two basic decisions: beneficiary and amount. Once individuals understand how to make a responsible grant, they will be on their way to understanding what is necessary to be responsible in making all their other financial decisions.

Multidimensional grant-making decisions

As already stated, grant making, like other financial transactions, requires multidimensional decisions. Each decision has more than one outcome. For example, when the decision is made to fund a grant, there is an impact on the cash flow budget established and perhaps a need to sell assets to create the cash necessary. The decision to fund one grant could cause other desired grants to be abandoned or get less support. Grant-making decisions also affect the relationships among those working in the grant-making entity. When they are family members, how a decision is made can have a significant impact on future decision making and family cohesiveness.

Organizers must consider the many dimensions of making a grant. Doing so is important to the long-term success of the effort—not only the success of the actual funding and subsequent program results but the development of the grant-making organization and its leaders.

Consequently, it is critical that a systematic approach and a participant-inclusive process be developed. Having developed such a process, grant makers can then apply it to personal and family financial stewardship as well.

An opportunity for mentoring

When we step back and look at the real issues faced by wealthy families and identify those that apply in specific circumstances, we normally see that each wealthy family faces several very difficult issues—some unique, but most universal. Universal challenges are often creating competent heirs, instilling in them the desire to be engaged in meaningful and character-building activities, helping them develop a positive sense of self, and encouraging them to stay connected with one another through a functioning family organization. The difficulty in meeting these challenges provides an opportunity for successful mentoring.

It is important to remember that the main purpose of the family is to support the personal development, growth, and well-being of the individual family members. Thus, it is important to have family members come together voluntarily rather than require participation. To paraphrase Kant, correct behavior will occur when institutions (in this case, families) are the means and individuals are the ends. Effective mentoring occurs when there is a desire to learn coupled with the will to teach.

The family organization can be the vehicle of choice for financial mentoring. It can accomplish that task through various shared experiences. Perhaps the best such experience, and the one most suited to youthful participation, is family philanthropic activity—primarily grant making. Grant-making-centered financial mentoring focuses on the nonpersonal benefits of wealth. It demonstrates the impact for good. It allows family members to experience the joy that wealth's impact on others can provide.

A grant-making organization provides unique and safe generation-to-generation coaching and mentoring in the area of financial stewardship. Perhaps most importantly, this mentoring process gives heirs experiences that foster personal growth and can lead to responsible behavior in all aspects of their lives.

For those who are naïve about budgets or investments, responsible grant making is the perfect way to learn about the due diligence process. Anyone involved in financial transactions can appreciate that meaningful due diligence prior to making a financial decision has enormous impact on the results. If this process is subsequently applied in all their major financial decisions, family members will be able to deal properly with all of their current and future oversight responsibilities.

Establishing the basis of responsible grant making

Grants to public charitable organizations serve donors in various ways: emotional, political, social, spiritual. They also serve donors' economic self-interests. Making a grant is not unlike going to the mall: choices are unlimited and appetites grow as the choices are presented. It could also be likened to dining at a buffet: people always seem to eat more when more is available. Human nature works the same way in the mall, at a buffet, and in grant making. In financial terms, our desire to consume can quickly outstrip our budget, regardless of the size of our budget.

In order to control our appetites, we must follow established guidelines. When we go out shopping, one such guideline could be always to bring a list. Another rule might be never to go to the grocery store when we are hungry. Whatever personal-planning guideline is established, it should normally cause better results if we follow it than if we do not. When it comes to financial decisions, going forward without such a guideline generally leads to disappointment in the outcome and may even result in a major failure.

Following that line of reasoning, it is necessary to create some form of *philanthropic statement of intent* in order to develop a set of responsible grant-making guidelines. The first step in creating that statement is to determine what the end result should look like. Participants also should articulate what they can do to achieve the desired result. Thus, the philanthropic statement of intent, which may also be called the statement of principles, mission statement, or values statement, will become the benchmark for creating guidelines that will help formulate decisions on what, how, and how much to give. This statement does not have to be long, but it should be comprehensive and understood by all who participate in the process.

For example, if it is determined that the underlying principle is that "people reach their maximum potential when they have the ability to act on versus being acted upon," then all grant-making decisions should promote that goal. Further defining the various ways that the statement of intent can be reached should take into consideration the lives of those who receive grants as well as those who make them.

The following is one family's philanthropic statement of intent:

The Family Philanthropic Fund has been set aside to promote and encourage the betterment of humanity by way of capital and time contributions from the members of the family. We want our contribution-participation to make an impact on the lives of others. We want to enrich their lives through education, new opportunities, or just by making them smile. In fulfilling this effort, special attention should be placed on encouraging individuals to be productive contributors to our society and do so in a manner that connects them with others.

What is a responsible grant?

Determining what makes for a responsible grant that will accomplish the statement of intent can be difficult and very subjective. What one person may feel is responsible, another may feel is irresponsible. What one person feels fulfills the statement of intent, another may think does not.

This subjective difference in opinion is further exacerbated when the grant is to be funded from one financial capital pool. It is especially the case when the various grantors are members of the same family organization, where decisions can become emotionally charged, competitive, and divisive. What would seem to be very clear-cut may become the subject of long-running disputes and resentments.

When parents establish the grant-making pool of financial capital they often expect the family to grow closer. They expect this noble effort to foster positive interactions. Although this may occur without coaching, most often the family must work at it. In order for this experience to be a positive one for participants, a compromise-based decision-making process must be developed, agreed upon, and followed. This process must be based on one or more underlying family values and principles that can be referred to when tensions develop. It must also appreciate and encourage the needs of each of the participating individuals. It must give them a venue of expression that is valued and recognized as such.

Attack the project, not the person suggesting it

For example, to provide a venue that is safe for all participants, it is important that the decisions made reflect the process and not personal opportunities. Using quantitative tools to reach decisions is helpful in achieving this important end.

The grant-making process must move, as much as possible, from the emotional realm to the factual realm. It is important to establish "reality checks" to draw discussions away from emotional interpretations. These reality checks should be done with each grant. The reality checks should focus on measurable outcomes. They should encourage dialogue instead of debate.

Responsible grant making should approach the effort in a manner that reduces the threat to each participant. It should set the stage for developing a problem-solving versus problem-creating method of communication.

Getting started in the due diligence process

The first sorting of grant requests is to determine which ones meet the areas agreed upon in the statement of intent. For example, if the statement of intent says that one objective is to "provide personal growth in individuals," it is important that this test be applied to each grant request to determine what level of personal growth it would encourage in the lives of recipients. Again, it is important to note that determining the level of personal growth that might take place is very subjective. There is a natural tendency to meet requests by favorite organizations by pushing what really does not match into a format that makes it seem to match. Responsible grant making requires tempering personal agendas. The philanthropic spirit of the effort must be maintained.

Each potential grantee organization should be asked to complete a standard data sheet that provides pertinent information about it and the purpose of grant. Such data sheets are available through many grant-making associations. Under a standard grant-request format, the requesting organization is responsible for providing the data. The data are normally assumed to be authentic.

Those that qualify under this initial review should then be subjected to a more comprehensive family-led data-gathering process. A participating family member should take the leadership role here.

This family leadership requirement sets the stage for control of the internal due diligence process. To make a grant responsibly, the family must gather further information beyond that provided by the grantee organization. This effort also begins the mentoring and training of the younger generations in the process of investigating before they invest. It provides the framework for the kind of due diligence efforts that will apply to both the investment of the philanthropic capital pool and the capital used by the family for its own purposes.

It can be quickly concluded that responsible grant making is a difficult task, one that requires significant oversight and investigation before going ahead. In order to assist in the decision-making effort, the development of a due diligence process that includes both qualitative and quantitative analysis for guiding the decision becomes critical.

The due diligence process begins with a previously-agreed-upon checklist. Exhibit 3.1 provides an example of the presentation information required when a proposal is made to the governing grant-making body. To be considered, a grant request must satisfy at least five of the listed items.

This second level of scrutiny will conclude with a site visit report by a family member. The opportunity for this family member is to

Exhibit 3.1. Strategic Grant-Making Decision Checklist

1. Will this grant provide a venue that brings our family closer together? How?
   a. _____
   b. _____
   c. _____
2. Does this grant promote personal growth for individuals? How?
   a. _____
   b. _____
   c. _____
3. Does this grant promote personal productivity? How?
   a. _____
   b. _____
   c. _____
4. Does this grant help those in need in a positive manner? How?
   a. _____
   b. _____
   c. _____
5. Does this grant satisfy the promotion of multiple core values held by our family? How?
   a. _____
   b. _____
   c. _____
6. Does the requested amount fall within our budget?
   Amount requested:_____
   Amount budgeted: _____

develop investigative and reporting skills. In addition, the family has the opportunity to see the skills and leadership abilities of each of its members. Some will do better than others. Some will rise to the occasion and others will not. This is exactly what is needed as future leadership is groomed and selected.

The following outline is an example of what a family member might look for during the follow-up site visit and review of the grant request. The family member should give leadership in determining the case for or against the organization requesting the grant. The report should include the following information:

Organization Background Information

1. A brief history and current operational status of the organization

   What are the apparent strengths (and weaknesses) of the personnel interviewed?
   What are the organization's barriers to achieving the results of the grant being requested?

2. A review of the organization's annual source and use of funds, particularly in the area in which the grant will be administered

   What is its ability to stay in business?
   Are there adequate operating reserves and a budget process that works?

3. A list of any complaints about this organization filed with the state attorney general and any other appropriate watchdog organization

4. A conversation with previous donors about their experience with the organization

   Were their expectations for the grant met? If not, why not?
   Do they plan to continue their support of the organization?

5. A review and assessment of the qualifications of the current leadership (board of directors, senior management, and personnel responsible for delivery of the services described in the grant request)

   What is the status of the current leadership?
   What is the leadership outlook for the next five years?
   Is there a program of leadership development?
   If the current leadership were to leave, who would assume that role?

6. General impressions from the site visit to the organization
7. The opinion of the reviewer of the ability of the organization to deliver the results proposed

Should the grant be made?

If the organization making the grant request passes this scrutiny, the next step is to determine how much of the requested funding will be approved. This decision is based on various leverage or capital preservation objectives of the statement of intent and staying within an approved annual budget. The following questions should be asked:

Funding Decision Review

1. Should the request be funded immediately or on a multiyear basis?
2. Should this grant be made as a matching grant?
3. Should it be done on a fractional funding to various checkpoints of accomplishment?
4. How does this grant affect our spending policy?
5. When do we make the agreed-upon grant payment?

Finally, in order to make the financial and nonfinancial decisions involved in a grant request, the family should devise some method for weighing all the inquiry data to reach a consensus decision. As noted earlier, the more the family employs quantitative decision-making tools, the easier it will be for them to achieve the desired outcomes. One way to do so is to create a grant approval calculator, shown in Exhibit 3.2. To be considered further, a grant request must get a score of twenty or higher.

Conclusion

The ability to discern between promotion and reality when dealing with grant requests or financial vendors comes with doing it. Much has been written about the need for fiduciaries to conduct a

Exhibit 3.2. Grant Approval Calculator

Question	*Ranking*
1. Does this grant fall within our mission statement?	1 2 3 4 5
2. Is the organization proposing this grant the best suited to implement it?	1 2 3 4 5
3. What is the quality of their accountability for this grant?	1 2 3 4 5
4. Does this grant fulfill our philanthropic objectives?	1 2 3 4 5
5. Can we afford it?	1 2 3 4 5
6. Does the structure of the grant provide engagement opportunities to the family that meet personal growth objectives?	1 2 3 4 5
Total score:	_____

Note: 1. We strongly disagree. 2. We feel somewhat favorable. 3. We feel favorable. 4. We feel more than favorable. 5. We strongly agree.

thorough due diligence process for their clients in investment management. It is not as easy to find information on how to do that due diligence. Most heads of family organizations struggle with the process of making a responsible grant, but it is similar in scope to making a good investment. Only the questions during inquiry will change.

Responsible grant making can occur only if a thoughtful and well-articulated statement of intent is created and an implementation process is developed and followed by family members. This process should be open to all family members. It should be conducted in such a manner that participants are not attacked. Instead, the emphasis should be on fulfilling agreed-upon objectives in the most effective, efficient, and consensual way. The process should encourage the emergence of future leadership.

If this process is followed, the family will prepare a succession plan for the management of not only its philanthropic activity but also its other financial affairs. The process will provide a venue for family engagement while promoting personal involvement on a voluntary basis. Remember, responsible grant making is multidimensional, offering benefits to the grantees as well as to the grantors. Both need to grow personally and develop in order for their lives to be enriched and fulfilled.

It is not only about money. . . . It is about people.

PAUL L. COMSTOCK *is chairman of the Paul L. Comstock Company in Houston, Texas.*

Can helping others be good for our health and well-being? This chapter summarizes recent research that offers new evidence in favor of this possibility.

4

An altruistic reanalysis of the social support hypothesis: The health benefits of giving

Stephanie L. Brown

WE TAKE FOR GRANTED that receiving support from our loved ones makes us feel good and keeps us healthy. Yet few studies have examined the alternative possibility that the "helper" also benefits from helping. Can helping others be good for our health and well-being? Recent attempts to study social influences on health offer new evidence in favor of this possibility. The purpose of this chapter is to summarize this research and describe a new "altruistic" way of thinking about close relationships that challenges current approaches to relationship science.

Background

Do social ties influence our health? Before 1988, many would have laughed at the question. "Of course not . . . unless you believe in magic," they would have chuckled. We take for granted that physical acts such as smoking, drinking, eating, and exercise affect our health. The possibility that social factors could also influence health

NEW DIRECTIONS FOR PHILANTHROPIC FUNDRAISING, NO. 42, WINTER 2003 © WILEY PERIODICALS, INC.

was not taken seriously until 1988 when James House, a professor of sociology at the University of Michigan, published a review paper in *Science* entitled, "Social Relationships and Health" (House, Landis, and Umberson, 1988). This revolutionary article was one of the first to elucidate the extensive evidence in favor of the possibility that social contact improves health and lengthens life. Fifteen years later, research continues to document that people who participate in high-quality social relationships are happier, healthier, and live longer than people who are socially isolated.

How does social contact influence health? The answer to this question may be just as much a mystery now as it was back in 1988. Researchers have tended to assume that people in close relationships receive more social support than their socially isolated counterparts (House, Landis, and Umberson, 1988). Despite the intuitive appeal of the assumption that receiving is good for our health, the evidence does not yield that conclusion. Tests of the hypothesis that receiving is beneficial have produced contradictory results (Smith, Fernengel, Holcroft, Gerald, and Marien, 1994), demonstrating in some instances that receiving support from others can be harmful (for example, Brown and Vinokur, in press). Some investigators have since challenged the receiving-support hypothesis, noting that there is a dark side to close relationships. Other researchers have shown that negative health problems arise when individuals get too much support. For example, Denys de Catanzaro, professor of psychology at McMaster University, and Michael Brown, professor of psychology at Pacific Lutheran University, have independently demonstrated that people who feel they are a burden to their loved ones are at risk for mental health problems such as depression, anxiety, and suicide (Brown, Dahlen, Mills, Rick, and Biblarz, 1999; de Catanzaro, 1986). If receiving support makes some people feel like a burden, then receiving could be harmful to, rather than improve, the health of the recipient.

After considering the limitations of the receiving-support hypothesis, I hypothesized that giving support, rather than receiving it, is what is beneficial about being in a close relationship. This idea derives from evolutionary biology and is consistent with social-psychological studies of helping and altruism. Evolutionary theories of altruism note the considerable importance of making a contribution to others (Hamilton, 1964; Trivers, 1971). We would not be around as a species if not for our willingness to provide for and protect our children, spouses, friends, neighbors, and relatives. It is this help we give that would have been crucial to our own reproductive success (for example, taking care of children) and to the success of those who shared our genes. Individuals may have been able to exert a strong influence over their own fitness—that is, the reproduction of their own genes—by fighting to stay alive and prolonging the amount of time that they could contribute to others.

If helping was adaptive for our ancestors, then it should be rewarding for us, or make us feel good at some level. This is certainly the implication of numerous studies that have examined the social-psychological basis for helping. Robert Cialdini, professor of psychology at Arizona State University, has been part of an ongoing debate with Daniel Batson, professor of psychology at the University of Kansas, over whether pure altruism exists (Batson, 1998). This debate has spawned a generation of research that documents the "egoistic" benefits of helping others. For example, helping has been associated with positive emotion, including relieving negative states such as sadness and distress. Positive emotion, in turn, has been shown by Barbara Fredrickson, professor of psychology at the University of Michigan, to speed recovery from cardiovascular stress—a known risk factor for mortality (Fredrickson, Mancuso, Branigan, and Tugade, 2000). If helping produces positive emotion, and positive emotion protects health, then helping may account for some of the health benefits of social contact.

Benefits of giving

To test the idea that helping others creates health benefits, I examined the data from the Changing Lives of Older Couples (CLOC) project with the help of Randolph Nesse, professor of psychiatry at the University of Michigan, Amiram Vinokur, professor of psychology there, and Dylan Smith, a research investigator in the school of medicine also at Michigan. The CLOC project was a study initiated a number of years ago by Camille Wortman, James House, Ronald Kessler, and Jim Lepkowski at the Institute for Social Research (Carr, House, Kessler, Nesse, Sonnega, and Wortman, 2000). The study followed a group of older couples for five years and was designed to look at psychological issues surrounding bereavement. Several factors made this study an ideal choice for examining the health benefits of giving. Most crucially, it included a tremendous number of high-quality measures of receiving *and giving* social support, and contained multiple measures of physical health, health behaviors, mental health, personality, and relationship dynamics. The study design allowed us to see how these variables related to later mortality.

Positive influence on longevity

We examined 423 couples and found that individuals who reported providing tangible forms of help to friends, relatives, and neighbors reduced their risk of dying by about one half, compared with individuals who reported providing no help to others. In addition, people who reported providing high amounts of emotional support to their spouse (for example, being willing to listen when the spouse needs to talk) were also about half as likely to die during the study period, compared with people who reported providing relatively lower amounts of emotional support. Receiving support had no influence on mortality.

These beneficial effects of giving remained after controlling for a variety of other factors that are typically associated with mortality risk—age, gender, socioeconomic status, race, self-rated health, functional health, smoking, drinking, exercise, depression, anxiety, subjective well-being, social contact (that is, how often individuals get together with friends or talk on the phone), dependence on one's partner—and individual differences, such as extroversion, agreeableness, locus of control, self-esteem, and emotional stability.

The results of this study offer preliminary support for the possibility that giving to others accounts for some of the health benefits of social contact. Because this is a single study, it is premature to conclude definitively that increasing what we give will improve our health and our longevity. But this is certainly the implication.

Other benefits of giving

Another study, also conducted on the CLOC sample, was designed to examine whether giving is protective for widows (Brown, Smith, House, and Brown, 2003). Results of this study demonstrated that (a) widows who gave instrumental support to others were less likely to have their grief develop into depressive symptoms one year later compared with widows who did not give instrumental support to others; (b) widows who increased their amount of giving had lower levels of depressive symptoms compared with widows who did not increase their amount of giving; (c) giving was associated with reduced depression over time for matched controls who did not lose a spouse. These findings were obtained after controlling for receiving support, social contact, religious involvement, physical health, and personality traits such as locus of control and self-esteem.

Similar findings have been obtained for dialysis patients. In a three-month longitudinal study of a peer-support intervention for dialysis patients, giving was associated with lower levels of depressive symptoms over time (Brown, Perry, and Swartz, 2003). A one-year study of dialysis patients demonstrated that when patients felt their caregiver needed them—which is potentially related to giving—it was protective as measured by fewer depressive symptoms and higher subjective well-being (Brown, Vinokur, Perry, and Swartz, 2003). Even among caregivers, giving appears to be beneficial to one's health. For example, giving was associated with lower levels of caregiver burnout and higher subjective well-being among caregivers of dialysis patients.

A new look at interpersonal relationships

If giving is important, adaptive, and good for our health and well-being, how do we become motivated to give in the first place? Previous work has shown that high-cost giving is a central feature of interpersonal relationships that are characterized by a social bond (Brown, 1999; Brown and Smith, 2003; Cialdini, Brown, Lewis, Luce, and Neuberg, 1997). As used here, a *bond* is defined as the experience of having feelings for another that involve affection, closeness, and commitment and that are enduring through time and in different contexts. Bonds are hypothesized to have been designed by natural selection to help individuals suppress their selfish tendencies so that they could reliably promote the well-being of another person. Giving behavior can be costly and maladaptive if it is directed indiscriminately, so it has been hypothesized further that bonds should have only formed under conditions that could not be exploited. These conditions are termed *fitness interdependence*, and refer to situations in which the fates of two or more individuals are intertwined. So, for example, individuals who were interdependent for fitness would have had common genes, common experiences, reciprocal exchanges, or the potential to have a child together. Because it entails a common fate, fitness interdependence would have provided a safety net, ensuring that giving behavior resulted in an increase rather than a decrease in reproductive success. If this is true, then we may tend to form bonds with individuals whom we need *and whom* we think *need us*.

Support for these ideas comes from a variety of disciplines, across a variety of giving behaviors such as sharing, self-sacrifice, and investing in young. For instance, studies of animal behavior note the selective occurrence of sharing and self-sacrifice among individuals who appear bonded to one another (de Waal, 1996). Anthropological ethnographies of human families illustrate that whether members of a particular society share outside the boundaries of the nuclear family is correlated with whether or not bonds exist between nonfamily members (Harrell, 1997). Findings from behavioral neuroendocrinology suggest that the hormonal basis of bonds is similar to that of parental investment. Specifically, experimental studies demonstrate that the hormones that underlie bonds (for example, oxytocin) also induce parental investment when injected into virgin animals who would otherwise kill unfamiliar young (Insel, 1993). Furthermore, the results from a direct test of the relationship between fitness interdependence, bonds, and giving demonstrated that fitness interdependence, bonds, and the desire to give at high cost could be measured as separable constructs (Brown, 1999; Brown and Smith, 2003). The results of this study demonstrated that bonds mediated the relationship between fitness interdependence and costly giving in different types of relationships, including biological relatives, romantic partners, and platonic friends. Thus, research is consistent with the possibility that bonds evolved to promote giving.

Because of its emphasis on altruistic functions, this "altruistic" view of interpersonal relationships is a radical departure from the prevailing tendency to emphasize the egoistic or individualistic benefits of maintaining a close relationship. For example, attachment theorists ask whether an infant can get its needs met from a parent or caregiver, social psychologists ask whether romantic relationships are satisfying to the individual, and health psychologists ask whether individuals receive enough social support from their relationship partners or from the community. Of the few research lines that pursue giving (for example, caregiving), the clear emphasis is on the stress and burnout that accompanies it as opposed to the possible value, meaning, or sense of "mattering" that may go along with it. The analysis presented here suggests that our affection for others (and our social nature more generally) may be rooted in the value of what we do for others, as opposed to what others do for us. If this is true, then satisfying romantic relationships may be those in which an individual feels she makes an important contribution to a partner, childhood attachment may require a child to feel useful to his parents, and the value of social support for health may depend as much (if not more) on what is given as on what is received.

Directions for future research

Several unanswered questions eagerly await future research. For example, is the motivation for giving different in bonded and non-bonded relationships (that is, in relationships that are interdependent rather than one-sided)? How much helping is optimal, and can too much be harmful? And are some types of helping more beneficial than others? We also need to know more about the precise mechanism through which helping others benefits health.

If the results of subsequent studies replicate and extend the present findings, then we may need to rethink the way we care for our loved ones. It may be that the best way to support other people is to provide them with an opportunity to feel useful—so that they can feel that they are making an important contribution to others.

References

Batson, C. D. "Altruism and Prosocial Behavior." In D.T. Gilbert, S.T. Fiske, and G. Lindzey (eds.), *Handbook of Social Psychology* (Vol. 2; pp. 282–316). New York: McGraw-Hill, 1998.

Brown, R. M., Dahlen, E., Mills, C., Rick, J., and Biblarz, A. "Evaluation of an Evolutionary Model of Self-Preservation and Self-Destruction." *Suicide and Life-Threatening Behavior*, 1999, *29* (1), 58–71.

Brown, S. L. *The Origins of Investment: A Theory of Close Relationships.* Unpublished dissertation, Arizona State University, 1999.

Brown, S. L., Perry, E., and Swartz, J. "Giving Support Reduces Depression Among Dialysis Patients." Unpublished manuscript, 2003.

Brown, S. L., and Smith, D. M. "Selective Investment Theory: Evidence That Different Types of Close Relationships Can Be Described by the Same Factor Structure." Unpublished manuscript, 2003.

Brown, S. L., Smith, D. M., House, J. S., and Brown, R. M. "Coping with Spousal Loss: The Buffering Effects of Giving Social Support to Others." Unpublished manuscript, 2003.

Brown, S. L., and Vinokur, A. D. "The Interplay Among Risk Factors for Suicidal Ideation and Suicide: The Role of Depression, Poor Health, and Loved Ones' Messages of Support and Criticism." *American Journal of Community Psychology*, in press.

Brown, S. L., Vinokur, A. D., Perry, E., and Swartz, J. "Burden May Be a Risk Factor for Declining Mental and Physical Health Among Dialysis Patients." Unpublished manuscript, 2003.

Carr, D., House, J. S., Kessler, R. C., Nesse, R. M., Sonnega, J., and Wortman, C. "Marital Quality and Psychological Adjustment to Widowhood Among Older Adults: A Longitudinal Analysis." *Journal of Gerontology*, 2000, *55B* (4), S197–S207.

Cialdini, R. B., Brown, S. L., Lewis, B. P., Luce, C., and Neuberg, S. L. "Reinterpreting the Empathy-Altruism Relationship: When One into One Equals Oneness." *Journal of Personality and Social Psychology*, 1997, *73*, 481–493.

de Catanzaro, D. "A Mathematical Model of Evolutionary Pressures Regulating Self-Preservation and Self-Destruction." *Suicide and Life-Threatening Behavior*, 1986, *16*, 166–181.

de Waal, F. *Good-Natured: The Origins of Right and Wrong in Humans and Other Animals.* Cambridge, Mass.: Harvard University Press, 1996.

Fredrickson, B., Mancuso, R., Branigan, C., and Tugade, M. "The Undoing Effect of Positive Emotions." *Motivation and Emotion*, 2000, *24*, 237–258.

Hamilton, W. D. "The Genetic Evolution of Social Behavior: I and II." *Journal of Theoretical Biology*, 1964, *7*, 1–52.

Harrell, S. *Human Families*. Boulder, Colo.: Westview Press, 1997.

House, J. S., Landis, K. R., and Umberson, D. "Social Relationships and Health." *Science*, 1988, *241*, 540–545.

Insel, T. R. "Oxytocin and the Neuroendocrine Basis of Affiliation." In J. Schulkin (ed.), *Hormonally Induced Changes in Mind and Brain*. San Diego: Academic Press, 1993.

Smith, C. E., Fernengel, K., Holcroft, C., Gerald, K., and Marien, L. "Meta-Analysis of the Associations Between Social Support and Health Outcomes." *Annals of Behavioral Medicine*, 1994, *16*, 352–362.

Trivers, R. L. "The Evolution of Reciprocal Altruism." *Quarterly Review of Biology*, 1971, *46*, 35–57.

STEPHANIE L. BROWN *is research investigator at the Institute for Social Research at the University of Michigan.*

We must move beyond the traditional thinking that older people are our past and younger people are our future. The potential and promise of both these populations must be found if we are to continue to build the legacy of volunteerism and philanthropy that is fundamental to our civil society.

5

Intergenerational service learning and volunteering

Donna M. Butts

WAKE UP AND SMELL the demographics. Older adults are living longer, are growing in numbers, and are healthier than ever before. Life expectancy in the United States increased from forty-seven years in 1900 to seventy-six in 1999. By 2050, it is expected to climb into the eighties. In addition, by the year 2030, the number of people over the age of sixty-five is expected to double to seventy million (Hobbs and Damon, 1996). The aging of the baby boom generation is so distinct that this generation has been labeled our country's fastest-growing natural resource.

At the same time, volunteering among high school students has reached its highest level in fifty years (INDEPENDENT SECTOR,

Note: Generations United represents more than a hundred national, state, and local organizations involving more than seventy million Americans. It is the only national organization advocating for the mutual well-being of children, youth, and older adults. Focused solely on promoting intergenerational strategies, programs, and public policies, it is a resource for policymakers and the public on the economic, social, and personal imperatives of intergenerational cooperation.

NEW DIRECTIONS FOR PHILANTHROPIC FUNDRAISING, NO. 42, WINTER 2003 © WILEY PERIODICALS, INC.

2002). Young people today are more likely to be engaged in one-to-one service on behalf of their communities than their predecessors were. Still, adolescence continues to be viewed by many as a "waiting place" for a generation that has not yet come of age and has little to offer. Similarly, as our demographics evolve, we are in danger of creating a new "waiting place" for an older generation cast off by many who see its members as burdensome individuals who are past their prime.

In reality we need to focus on re-creating service opportunities to capture the power of both young and old as volunteers and philanthropists. We must move beyond the traditional thinking that older people are our past and younger people are our future. The potential and promise of both of these populations can and must be found today if we are to continue to build the legacy of volunteerism and philanthropy that is fundamental to our civil society.

This chapter discusses the important role of intergenerational approaches in fostering engagement that lasts throughout the life span. Philanthropy, civic engagement, and service learning are intertwining opportunities, invaluable vehicles through which to connect people of all generations to their communities. The term *philanthropy* is often defined as voluntary action for the public good. Philanthropy is directed to improving the quality of life and fostering preservation of values through giving of time, money, or association. In other words, the term *philanthropy* extends beyond simple financial contributions to include contributions that can be made through volunteer and service learning programs.

Today's changing demographics

The late psychologist Erik Erikson expressed his theory of generativity in the phrase, "I am what survives of me." In the 1950s, men retired at about age sixty-seven and women at about sixty-eight (Employee Benefits Research Institute, 2001). Today the age is much lower: around sixty-two for men and sixty-one for women. Although the retirement age is decreasing, a recent study indicates that when they retire, 80 percent of boomers do not intend to do so in any traditional way (Civic Ventures, 2002). They see retirement as a time to begin a new chapter, not close the book. These younger, healthier "new old" are demanding different lifestyles from the generations that preceded them. Most will work part-time or seek meaningful volunteer opportunities, with 70 percent saying they want to try new things and 81 percent reporting they want to continue to learn. Rather than move to the sun belt, 73 percent say they want to continue to live in the age-integrated communities in which they have worked and lived.

Unfortunately, despite these trends, older people in the United States are more likely to be seen as a triad of needs—social security, Medicare, and prescription drugs. Many look at the older population as a burden. Yet, in fact, in 2000 only 4.5 percent of the older adult population resided in nursing homes ("Living Arrangements of the Elderly," 2003). The reality is that older adults are often actively giving care rather than receiving it. The 2000 census revealed that 2.1 million grandparents have sole responsibility for raising grandchildren. A recent Census Bureau study found that 21 percent of preschool-age children were taken care of by their grandparents, freeing up the middle generation to work (U.S. Census Bureau, 2002).

At the same time, INDEPENDENT SECTOR reports that 59.3 percent of teens between the ages of twelve and seventeen volunteer, and 70 percent of teens participate in activities to improve their communities. Professionals in the youth field have made progress in shifting the way communities view youth. Positive youth development provides a framework for engaging youth as resources and true partners in civic life. Rather than viewing young people as problems to be solved, more opportunities are being created for them to exercise and demonstrate their leadership abilities. Such opportunities help them develop a range of skills, including critical thinking, writing, public speaking, planning, and group dynamics (Mohamed and Wheeler, 2001). For example, one advantage of young people participating in philanthropy, according to the Coalition of Community Foundations for Youth, is that it can make philanthropic values, principles, and traditions come alive for them and their communities. Youth involved in these types of programs continue to volunteer their time, contribute money to charitable causes, and serve in leadership positions at higher rates than the general population. Indeed, two-thirds of today's adult volunteers report they began volunteering when they were young (Graza and Stevens, 2002).

Coupled with the fact that more state and local initiatives are requiring youth to perform community service to meet graduation requirements, these opportunities, if thoughtfully undertaken, can encourage lifelong habits of civic engagement and philanthropy.

Current interest in civic engagement and service learning

Peter Hart's 2002 research report on retirement found that people between the ages of fifty-five and sixty-four wanted substantial, meaningful volunteer opportunities, not just something to take up their time. The report went on to say, "Civic engagement is about filling a need to both make a difference and be involved" (Peter D. Hart Research Associates, 2002). Engaging older adults and young people in volunteerism and philanthropy requires developing mechanisms and opportunities that have substance and that profit from their unique skills. Both groups are more likely to be motivated to participate and contribute when they are involved in all stages of program development. Young and old are more likely to succeed if they are well prepared for the experience, educated in advance, and supported during the process.

Knowing that they can make a concrete change in the community is motivational for both generations. Intergenerational service learning programs offer both this opportunity. Service learning programs are school- or community-based efforts in which learners of all ages learn and develop through active participation in community service. By design, service learning programs involve more structure and a greater commitment than traditional volunteer experiences. The emphasis is put equally on the service and the learning aspects of the program. The activities are integrated into and enhance the curriculum or educational components of the school or community-based program and provide time for reflection. Communities are also strengthened as often-overlooked generations—that is, new resources—are engaged (Generations United, 2002a).

Some background on intergenerational programs and service learning

Intergenerational service learning programs are one component of a growing intergenerational field. The roots of intentional intergenerational programs can be traced back to the days of the War on Poverty. The first documented program, the federally sponsored Foster Grandparent Program, began in 1965, when low-income older adults were recruited to work with young children who had special or exceptional needs. The program was deemed valuable because the volunteers received a stipend that helped them with their living expenses, as well as health care coverage, in exchange for their hours of service. In addition, the program was thought to help address a new concern: the growing isolation of the old and the increasing separation between the generations.

Over the next three and a half decades many small community-based intergenerational programs of all kinds developed. Today there are hundreds, perhaps thousands, of such programs under way in rural and urban communities across the country. Hampered by stereotypes, they are often viewed as nice but not very relevant, sweet but without substance. During the last decade, however, more communities have come to understand that intergenerational programs are quite substantive—far more than the annual birthday visit to the nursing home by local grade school children. They are sustained interventions that draw on the unique strengths of each generation.

In addition, intergenerational programs provide a venue for regular contact between the generations and encourage people of different generations to be advocates for each other. For example, seniors volunteering in a school in Oregon were dismayed by the lack of supplies there. They went to the school board to testify that "their children" needed more resources. This is a far cry from the picture that many have of senior citizens organizing to defeat funding measures for public schools.

Intergenerational service learning programs offer a venue to engage young and old in service to their communities, unlike other program models that cast them in service only to each other. For example, a traditional intergenerational tutoring program might involve an older person working in an elementary school with a child or a group of children. An intergenerational service learning program might involve three generations—a high school student tutoring a grade-school child while also working with an older volunteer to plan lessons, research literacy programs, and reflect together on the service they are providing.

Service learning itself is not a new concept. It first emerged in the late nineteenth and early twentieth centuries. John Dewey believed that students would learn more effectively and become better citizens if they engaged in community service as part of their academic curriculum (Generations United, 2002a). It was not until the 1970s, however, that service learning started to take hold, and it was even later that the concept began to be widely implemented. Still, the quality of the programs varies. In *Young and Old Serving Together: Meeting Community Needs Through Intergenerational Partnerships*, Generations United (2002a) recommends six guiding principles when implementing service learning programs:

- Reciprocity is essential.
- Activities meet real community needs.
- Reflection is planned.
- Partnerships created by the program build community.
- Careful planning and preparation are vital.
- Young and old are involved as decision makers.

Some experts view intergenerational community service as a vehicle for building support for public schools, raising awareness about the environment and public safety, and helping all community members, young and old, live healthier lifestyles. The experiences assist with the transfer of learning between school and nonschool environments, proving that institutions can help shape the civic-engagement behaviors of tomorrow's adults. Through joint community service, both young and old are seen as members of an enduring historical community, one that existed before their birth and will remain after their departure. The benefits of their work reach beyond the needs and interests of the very young and the very old to enrich society as a whole (Moody and Disch, 1989).

New opportunities

Although interest in civic engagement and intergenerational service learning are increasing, development of the systems needed to support them has not kept pace. Gone are the days when older and younger volunteers were content to rock babies in nurseries. Some still do, but now these volunteers are more likely to want to rock the boat. They want to serve on the board, help plan the program, and make decisions that use their enthusiasm, experience, or education. And although more school districts are requiring "hours of service" to qualify for graduation, community-based options are limited, often because the number of hours mandated are so few. For instance, one school district in California requires nine hours of community service. Unless this time is carefully planned, it is hardly enough to become fully committed to a project and not nearly enough to warrant a program sponsor's investment.

Several programs exist for senior volunteers, administered through the Senior Corps of the Corporation for National and Community Service. Most of these, however, including the Foster Grandparents and Retired and Senior Volunteer Program, have not been recast to involve the changing senior population effectively. The poverty guidelines under which they were established might have made sense forty years ago, but today they are outdated and need to be revisited so that they can successfully recruit qualifying older adults. To their advantage, these programs do offer a small stipend to the volunteers, which is something not currently available to low-income youth who may want to volunteer but lack the resources to do so.

At the same time, the bridge from work to retirement is under construction. Challenging volunteer experiences that engage older adults with a wide range of interests are limited. Life Option Centers is one evolving concept to help address this issue. Developed by Civic Ventures, a nonprofit that works to expand opportunities for older Americans to contribute to society, these centers are designed to recognize the fundamental importance of building programs and services that are accessible, culturally sensitive, and connected to the larger community. They are designed to leverage organizational resources to create a common ground, learning resources, and access to information for transitions that link people in their middle and older years to the life of the community and its needs. To appeal to an older population, the creators recommend redefining volunteering as "working for the city" or "working in the public interest" to help elevate the image of service (Civic Ventures & Libraries for the Future, 2003).

However the opportunities are defined—whether as youth or senior engagement—communities can be better prepared to embrace the "bookend generations" if they begin to look through an intergenerational lens. Intentionally using the filter of young and old can help communities identify advisory boards, programs, and physical spaces that could be enhanced by adding an intergenerational component. For example, a food bank in rural Kansas may have a history of older volunteers helping to prepare and deliver food boxes to needy families. That same program could recruit students from a local high school to work side by side with the senior volunteers after school. Rich discussion would occur while the team is involved with packaging food and planning delivery routes. Learning would be enhanced for both generations if a rest and reflection period were added at the end of the workday.

An additional opportunity for connecting the generations for the good of the community exists in the growing interest in intergenerational shared sites. Young and old share the common bond of neighborhood. The worlds they inhabit are more likely to have much narrower boundaries than the ages between them. However, because neighborhoods and local facilities are often age-segregated, there is little opportunity for natural interaction. Senior centers, child care centers, and schools are examples of physical spaces that are rich in potential that can be tapped in a variety of ways. Intergenerational shared-site programs serve multiple generations and offer planned as well as informal interactions and programs that connect the generations. Shared sites include indoor and outdoor spaces designed and built specifically for children, youth, and older adults. Common models include child care centers housed in nursing homes, where there are interactive, planned activities, or schools with embedded senior centers (Generations United, 2002b). Shared sites offer proximity and encourage natural interaction and activity. They provide fertile ground for nurturing the values of philanthropy and service learning.

Transferring values

As already noted, involvement in philanthropy and volunteerism is a lifelong habit that can be cultivated through intergenerational learning experiences. Whether in the context of family or in partnership with other caring adults, those who volunteered as youth give and volunteer more as adults than those who did not (Generations United, 2002b). Although intergenerational programs provide important connections between unrelated members of different generations, families have a unique responsibility to cultivate good philanthropic habits. One couple, for instance, sets aside one hundred dollars each year and then spends an evening with their children discussing community issues, reviewing funding appeals, and reading newspaper clippings spotlighting local social service programs. Together they determine how their philanthropic funds should be distributed. As a family, they carry this one important step further by visiting the programs, delivering their checks in person, and often volunteering at the same time. The children look forward to this annual event. They have learned that all people, no matter how large or small their assets, can be philanthropists. They have also connected their contributions with real programs and people, humanizing what may seem to be a very sterile process.

Conclusion

In order for any society to progress and prosper, each generation must provide assistance to, and receive assistance from, those that follow. This assistance includes sharing the values of philanthropy, service learning, volunteerism, and civic engagement. The reciprocity of giving and receiving that goes on over time among individuals, and between generations, becomes a commanding principle. Our social compact is the bond of interdependence that ties society together (Kingson, Hirshorn, and Cornman, 1986). Anyone who has been involved with an intergenerational program knows there is tremendous power when young and old are united in meaningful, purposeful work. Together they build healthier, safer, more inclusive communities, and in the end, make our country stronger. These programs are strength-based, reciprocal, and respectful of all ages. As a member of Generations United once said, "If you take the potential of youth, the experience of age, and mix them together, what do you get? *Dynamite.*" It is the spark that can change the world.

References

Civic Ventures. *New Face of Retirement: An Ongoing Survey of American Attitudes on Aging.* San Francisco: Civic Ventures, 2002.

Civic Ventures & Libraries for the Future. *Life Options Blueprint.* San Francisco: Civic Ventures, 2003. [www.civicventures.org/site/life_options/loc_blueprint_6_4_3.pdf].

Employee Benefits Research Institute. *Trends in Early Retirement.* Washington, D.C.: Employee Benefits Research Institute, 2001.

Generations United. *Young and Old Serving Together: Meeting Community Needs Through Intergenerational Partnerships.* Washington, D.C.: Generations United, 2002a.

Generations United. *Reaching Across the Ages: An Action Agenda to Strengthen Communities Through Intergenerational Shared Sites and Shared Resources.* Washington, D.C.: Generations United, 2002b.

Graza, P., and Stevens, P. *Best Practices in Youth Philanthropy.* Basehor, Kan.: Coalition of Community Foundations for Youth, 2002.

Hobbs, F. B., and Damon, B. L. "65+ in the United States." *Current Population Reports* (Special Studies, P23–190). Washington, D.C.: Bureau of the Census and the National Institute on Aging, 1996. [www.census.gov/prod/1/pop/p23–190.html].

INDEPENDENT SECTOR. *Engaging Youth in Lifelong Service.* Washington, D.C.: INDEPENDENT SECTOR, 2002. [www.independentsector.org/programs/research/engagingyouth.html].

Kingson, E. R., Hirshorn, B., and Cornman, J. *Ties That Bind: The Interdependence of Generations.* Washington, D.C.: Seven Locks Press, 1986.

"Living Arrangements of the Elderly"(press release). Washington, D.C.: Administration on Aging, 2003. [www.aoa.dhhs.gov/prof/statistics/profile.html].

Mohamed, I. A., and Wheeler, W. *Broadening the Bounds of Youth Development: Youth as Engaged Citizens.* New York: Innovation Center for Community and Youth Development and the Ford Foundation, 2001.

Moody, H. R., and Disch, R. "Intergenerational Programming in Public Policy." In S. Newman and S. W. Brummel (eds.), *Intergenerational Programs: Imperatives, Strategies, Impacts, Trends* (pp. 101–110). New York: Hawthorne Press, 1989.

Peter D. Hart Research Associates. *New Face of Retirement.* Washington, D.C.: Peter D. Hart Research Associates, 2002. [www.civicventures.org].

U.S. Census Bureau. "Who's Minding the Kids?" (press release). Washington, D.C.: U.S. Census Bureau, 2002. [www.uscensus.gov/pressrelease/www/2002/cb02–102.html].

DONNA M. BUTTS *is executive director of Generations United in Washington, D.C.*

*The Center on Philanthropy Panel Study (COPPS)
reports on the giving and volunteering of more than
seventy-four hundred households in 2001 and 2003
and the households' composition, income, and wealth
over the previous thirty years. These data will help
researchers and fundraisers understand many
aspects of philanthropy not previously understood.*

6

Tracking giving across generations

Richard Steinberg, Mark Wilhelm

WHAT EFFECT DOES PARENTAL ROLE MODELING have on the philanthropic behaviors of their adult children? When adult children
inherit their parents' wealth, are they as generous with this money
as they are with their own earnings? These are two of the questions
we are trying to answer using a wonderful new data source, the
Center on Philanthropy Panel Study (COPPS). This study reports on
the giving and volunteering of more than seventy-four hundred
households in 2001 and 2003 and the households' composition,
income, and wealth over the previous thirty years. These data will
help researchers and fundraisers understand many new aspects of
philanthropy. In this chapter we describe these data and the many

Note: We are grateful to Ted Flack for suggesting ways practitioners might use these
data. Richard Steinberg thanks the Centre for Nonprofit and Philanthropic Studies at
Queensland Institute of Technology for their hospitality during the writing of this
chapter. We also are grateful to The Atlantic Philanthropies for providing the financial support necessary to launch the *Center on Philanthropy Panel Study* (COPPS).
COPPS results from a partnership between the Center on Philanthropy at Indiana University and the Survey Research Center at the University of Michigan.

NEW DIRECTIONS FOR PHILANTHROPIC FUNDRAISING, NO. 42, WINTER 2003 © WILEY PERIODICALS, INC.

questions they can help to answer. We focus on two types of questions—those relating to giving across generations, and those relating to improving fundraising practice.

The Center on Philanthropy Panel Study

In contrast to an annual series of cross-sectional surveys in which a different random sample of respondents is selected for each year's survey, a panel study selects a random sample in the first year and then reinterviews those same respondents year after year. COPPS is part of a larger data collection project—the *Panel Study of Income Dynamics* (PSID) conducted by the Survey Research Center at the University of Michigan.

Since its initial interview year in 1968, the PSID has become the nation's longest-running, nationally representative social science panel survey. Although the primary focus of data collection is economic and demographic, also included are health, social, and psychological indicators. The PSID has been used in more than two thousand scientific studies and is the only social science project to make the National Science Foundation's "nifty fifty" list of the fifty projects that have had important effects on everyday life.

In 2001 COPPS added a series of questions on giving and volunteering to the PSID's rich database. The questions ask about amounts given for several charitable purposes: religious, combined funds, basic needs (poverty relief), health, education, youth and family services, the arts, neighborhoods, the environment, and international aid. There are also questions about volunteering. Both series were expanded for the 2003 wave, and we hope to continue these series indefinitely in future waves of the PSID.

Although there are other notable data sets on giving and volunteering, none combine the advantages of COPPS as a panel survey linked to a broader and longer-term panel. First, panel data have become the gold standard across social science disciplines for detecting cause-and-effect relationships. Suppose that, say, higher levels of income are associated with higher levels of giving. This hints that one causes the other, but it certainly does not prove the point. With panel data, the analyst can see whether respondents who personally enjoyed an increase in income gave more following that increase, and this is far more persuasive evidence of cause and effect.

Second, COPPS lets analysts study giving and volunteering over the life course. Panel data follow the same households over time, tracing their entire life histories. Third, COPPS permits intergenerational analysis of giving and volunteering. This is because the PSID employs "genealogical sampling," continuing to interview adult children after they leave their households of origin. Fourth, COPPS supplements data on giving and volunteering with a broad range of high-quality contextual data, including income, wealth, work hours, wages, health, family structure, and demographic data. Such data are usually unavailable in other surveys of giving and volunteering; in the PSID they stretch back thirty-three years. Finally, with a sample of 7,406 households, COPPS is more than twice the size of the next largest survey of giving and volunteering in the United States. Thus, the size of any effects on giving can be more precisely and reliably measured.

One of us compared the quality of data from the first wave of COPPS with that in five other studies of giving in the United States (Wilhelm, 2003). He found that COPPS provides the highest-quality data since the *National Study of Philanthropy* (NSP) in 1974. The NSP, fielded as part of the Filer Commission report, oversampled high-income households and so is generally thought to have the most accurate survey estimates of giving at the high end. (The Commission on Private Philanthropy & Public Needs—known as the Filer Commission, after Chairman John H. Filer—was formed in 1973 to study private philanthropy and its relationship with government.) COPPS data were closer than that provided by the other four surveys to NSP giving by the most generous 10 percent of respondents. The same was true in comparing COPPS with income tax data, which also accurately track high-end giving. In addition, COPPS excelled in two other dimensions: a high survey response rate and a dramatically lower occurrence of item nonresponse to the questions about amounts given.

Giving across generations

Table 6.1 provides an illustration of the type of question that can be answered using COPPS data. Here, we report differences in giving across three generations: prewar (born 1945 or earlier), baby boom (born 1946 to 1964), and generation X (born 1965 and after). The respective age categories in 2001 were fifty-six and older, thirty-seven to fifty-five, and thirty-six and younger. We report overall differences, differences in giving to religious organizations for religious purposes, and differences in giving to "secular" organizations (which include religiously affiliated hospitals, schools, and social service agencies as well as gifts to all organizations not affiliated with a religion).

Giving levels vary across generations for many reasons. For example, the average prewar respondent is wealthier than the average generation X respondent, so it is not surprising that the former would give more. However, we have tried to adjust the survey results statistically to remove the impact of wealth and many other differences to get at a pure generational effect. Table 6.1 reports

Table 6.1. Giving Across Generations

	Prewar	Baby Boom	Generation X
Any gift	$1,764.0[x,b]	$1,254.0[p]	$1,100.0[p]
Gift to religious organization	$1,169.0[x,b]	$752.0[p]	$660.0[p]
Other (nonreligious) gift	$595.0	$501.0	$440.0

Note: Details of this calculation are reported in Steinberg and Wilhelm, 2003. Statistical significance levels are reported as superscripts: x indicates the value for this generation is significantly different from the value for generation X, p indicates a difference from the prewar generation, and b indicates a difference from baby boomers. Difference shown is at the .001 level.

Source: Steinberg and Wilhelm, 2003.

predicted levels of giving per person if everyone in the sample were a member of the indicated generation but retained their other characteristics (family income, wealth, sex of family head, marital status, number of children, age of youngest child, employment status, health, race, ethnicity, region, city size, education, and religious affiliation). Thus, if everyone in the sample were members of the prewar generation gifts per person would be about $1,764; if all were baby boomers they would be about $1,254; and if all were of generation X they would be about $1,100.

The difference between the prewar and later generations is striking, suggesting that later generations are about one-third less generous. This difference is both numerically large and statistically significant—which means we would very rarely see such large differences in other samples unless average generosity really did differ across generations. Baby boomers seem a bit more generous than generation Xers, but this difference is small and not statistically significant.

In the second and third rows of Table 6.1, we see how the generations differ in giving to religious versus nonreligious organizations. The striking result is that almost all the dropoff in giving by the later generations is the result of a decline in religious giving. Giving to other causes differs little across the generations, and the small differences reported in Row 3 are not statistically significant. To interpret these results, we should be clear on the precise definitions of both categories. Respondents were asked "Did you make any donations specifically for religious purposes or spiritual development—for example to a church, synagogue, mosque, TV, or radio ministry? Please do not include donations to schools, hospitals, and other charities run by religious organizations. I will be asking you about those donations next" (*Panel Study of Income Dynamics*, 2001). This was recorded as a religious gift. Nonreligious giving is everything else: donations to combined funds (for example, United Way, Catholic Charities, United Jewish Appeal, and so on), to help people with basic needs, for health care purposes, for educational purposes, to youth and family services, for improving neighborhoods, to the arts, for the environment, for international aid, and for open-ended purposes that respondents might mention. These were reported separately, but are combined in the present chapter. Although these latter organizations are nonreligious in the sense that their primary purpose is not worship or spiritual development, donors may consider religious affiliation in deciding whether to support them.

Table 6.2 reports on giving by generation in much greater detail. The first row shows the share of respondents who made a gift. Thus, 80 percent of respondents of the prewar generation made gifts totaling at least $25 (those making smaller gifts were not queried further). Baby boomers were similar, with 75 percent making a gift, and only 53 percent of generation Xers giving. This means that it makes a great difference whether we report the average gift by someone who is a donor (Row 3) or by all respondents (Row 2), because the latter category includes many zero values in the average. We can now split the generational differences into two parts: the part due to reduced likelihood of making a gift, and the part due to reduced size of gifts by donors. We see that boomers who give, give almost the same amount as prewar donors ($2,222 versus $2,269), so the difference in average giving between these generations is mostly due to the lower proportion of givers in the former generation (75 percent versus 80 percent). In contrast, gen-Xers are both less likely to give and less generous when they do give.

A few donors make enormous gifts, and these gifts have great impact on the reported average. Thus, we also report the median gift for all respondents (Row 4) and for donors (Row 5). The median gift is the gift reported by the middle guy, in that half the sample gave a larger amount and half a smaller amount. Because there is no ceiling on the largest gift that can be made, but there is a floor (even the stingiest cannot give less than nothing), the median gift is much lower than the average. To capture high-end giving, we also report giving by donors in the ninety-fifth percentile (Row 6). Only 5 percent of the respondents made larger gifts than the values reported in this row.

Table 6.2. Giving Across Generations: Details

	Everyone	Prewar	Baby Boom	Generation X
Any gift				
Percent who give	69.0%	80.0%	75.0%	53.0%
Sample average gift (includes nongivers)	$1,328.0	$1,788.0	$1,662.0	$532.0
Sample average gift (excludes nongivers)	$1,942.0	$2,269.0	$2,222.0	$1,025.0
Sample median gift (includes nongivers)	$303.0	$620.0	$500.0	$40.0
Sample median gift (excludes nongivers)	$775.0	$1,080.0	$928.0	$400.0
Sample 95th percentile (includes nongivers)	$5,600.0	$6,386.0	$6,700.0	$3,000.0
Number in sample	4,616	1,117	2,008	1,491
Predicted average gift (includes nongivers)	$1,328.0	$1,764.0	$1,254.0	$1,100.0
Gift to religious organization				
Percent who give	47.0%	62.0%	51.0%	31.0%
Sample average gift (includes nongivers)	$823.0	$1,168.0	$991.0	$339.0
Sample average gift (excludes nongivers)	$1,744.0	$1,888.0	$1,936.0	$1,099.0
Sample median gift (includes nongivers)	$0.0	$300.0	$50.0	$0.0
Sample median gift (excludes nongivers)	$700.0	$1,000.0	$960.0	$300.0
Sample 95th percentile (includes nongivers)	$4,255.0	$5,000.0	$5,000.0	$2,200.0
Number in sample	4,616	1,117	2,008	1,491
Predicted average gift (includes nongivers)	$823.0	$1,169.0	$752.0	$660.0
Other (nonreligious) gift				
Percent who give	57.0%	66.0%	63.0%	44.0%
Sample average gift (includes nongivers)	$504.0	$620.0	$671.0	$193.0
Sample average gift (excludes nongivers)	$878.0	$940.0	$1,064.0	$441.0
Sample median gift (includes nongivers)	$60.0	$115.0	$130.0	$0.0
Sample median gift (excludes nongivers)	$325.0	$350.0	$400.0	$200.0
Sample 95th percentile (includes nongivers)	$2,000.0	$2,300.0	$2,550.0	$900.0
Number in sample	4,616	1,117	2,008	1,491
Predicted average gift (includes nongivers)	$504.0	$595.0	$502.0	$439.0

Source: Steinberg and Wilhelm, 2003.

How does one generation affect giving by the next?

At gatherings of philanthropic practitioners, the question "How can parents most effectively encourage the development of their children's philanthropic values?" is a surefire discussion starter. Most practitioners have formed opinions about this based on their family's experience, the experiences of friends, and perhaps, their professional experience providing advice to philanthropists who want to pass their values on to their children. Advice is also available from the many books on children and money (for example, Gallo and Gallo, 2002). During the December holidays, the *New York Times* runs feature stories in which families describe how they are passing on philanthropic traditions to their children.

Social scientists also are interested in how helping behavior develops in children, and in particular, the role parents play in that development. Much of what is known about the development of children's helping behavior comes from the developmental psychology literature. However, this literature concerns short-term behavior in laboratory settings, and one wonders whether results carry over into adult behaviors resulting from real-world experiences.

Philanthropic practitioners are, of course, ultimately interested in donations made during adulthood. However, much less is known about how parents affect the adulthood giving of their children because the data necessary to conduct nationally representative studies are extremely expensive to collect. There are two reasons for this: (1) data have to be collected from both parents and their adult children, and (2) a wide range of information must be collected. COPPS provides a wealth of information, enabling researchers to make some progress here.

We are currently involved in two research projects that explore parental influences on the giving of their adult children. Neither study is complete at this time, and so we do not report results here. In the first (Wilhelm, Brown, Rooney, and Steinberg, 2003), we estimate the strength of the relationship between the current giving of parents and their adult children. Half the group of adult children in COPPS whose parents are still alive and participating in the survey are baby boomers and half are generation Xers. In the second (Steinberg, Wilhelm, Brown, and Rooney, 2003), we examine how adult children spend their inheritances. Specifically, we estimate the parents' propensity to make annual gifts out of their own wealth and compare this with the adult children's propensity to give out of their inherited wealth. This will let us see whether the coming large wealth transfer (Havens and Schervish, 1999) is likely to increase or decrease annual giving.

Using COPPS to advance the practice of fundraising

Obviously, there is much more to learn from COPPS about patterns of giving. In the remainder of this chapter we speculate on how the results from future studies could be used to improve the practice of fundraising. We suggest that there are potential uses in *targeting* solicitation efforts, *predicting* the effect of changes in the economy or public policy on giving, *benchmarking* the success of campaigns, and *persuading* donors that their gifts will not endanger their financial health over the life cycle. Unlike internal studies using proprietary data about the success of individual campaigns, these studies will produce evidence derived from the experience of multiple campaigns that can be shared with the fundraising community.

Targeting

Campaign efforts are expensive. Donor markets are often segmented, and everything possible should be done to direct efforts toward those segments of the market most likely to respond positively. Existing studies tell us a lot about patterns of giving across donors at a point in time. We know that on average, those with higher income, wealth, level of education, and age give more than others. But we do not know, for example, whether this generosity is due to higher levels of income or to some hidden trait that makes the donor both earn more and give more. Thus, we do not know to what extent someone whose own income goes up will give more, and so do not know for sure that those whose incomes suddenly increase are good prospects for new solicitation efforts. Studies using COPPS will allow us to follow individual donors as these factors change while their hidden traits remain constant, and so learn the real indicators of generosity.

In addition, COPPS will reveal the characteristics of donors who give regularly, year after year. This understanding can be used to direct prospecting efforts toward those who will respond not just once but many times in the future. Further, COPPS can be used to figure out the lifetime value of gifts made by donors having different characteristics.

COPPS will also allow us to study the history of giving to each of the surveyed causes and learn more about the likely success of mailing lists derived from giving to other causes. For instance, suppose we found that those who give to the arts for the first time are more likely to give for educational purposes two years later but no more likely to give for religious purposes two years later. Then mailing lists of new donors to the arts would be a good purchase for those prospecting for new education donors and a poor purchase for those prospecting for new donors for religious purposes.

Finally, COPPS allows us to study the effect of many factors not included in other available surveys. For example, there is extensive detail on the history of the various components of wealth and income. There are measures of expenditures on housing, automobiles, and other components of household consumption. Therefore, COPPS can be used to ask whether these components are correlated with charitable giving. Moreover, the data allow us to learn whether those who take higher financial risks are more or less likely to donate, and whether those recovering from bankruptcy are good prospects. Besides expenditure data, there are data on the make and model of the family's cars and whether these cars were purchased new or used. If these factors are correlated with any aspect of giving, the application to targeting is immediate.

Predicting

How does a local disaster affect local giving to various causes? How do changes in state laws on the regulation, accountability, and taxation of organizations affect giving in that state? Currently, the only way to learn the answer is to live through such a change. However, the COPPS sample is large enough that we can obtain reliable information at the state level for many states. To the extent this information is transferable, we can improve our ability to predict giving outcomes. For example, from learning how donors to each cause and in each income class react to, say, an earthquake in California or a scandal involving nonprofit hospitals in New York, we can predict how donors in other states will react to similar changes, and do so at the time the change first occurs.

Benchmarking

How do your donors compare with donors to other charities serving related purposes? Is the difference the result of differences in the income, wealth, and other characteristics of your donor pool or of problems or successes in your campaign? COPPS data provide generalizable information on average giving for donor pools with the characteristics of your campaign and those of comparison campaigns. From the history of giving, you can benchmark whether your donors are upgrading their annual gifts at rates comparable to other campaigns, after adjusting for differences in donor pools.

Persuading

Rosenberg (1994) points out that the chief barrier to increased giving by the wealthy is unwarranted fear of financial misfortune. Donors are afraid that too much giving will deplete their wealth. He also argues that this fear is excessive, and that most donors could give far more without endangering their ability to enjoy retirement and pass on wealth to their heirs. COPPS can be used to generate more evidence to persuade donors that their fear is excessive because it can illustrate how the wealth of real donors changed over the lifetime following major gifts. The data are not ideal for this purpose,

because COPPS has a representative sample including only a few
wealthy donors, but this may suffice to assuage donor anxiety.

References

Gallo, E., and Gallo, J. *Silver Spoon Kids: How Successful Parents Raise Responsible Children.* Chicago: Contemporary Books, 2002.
Havens, J., and Schervish, P. "Millionaires and the Millennium: New Esti-
mates of the Forthcoming Wealth Transfer and Prospects for a Golden Age
of Philanthropy" (Social Welfare Research Institute working paper). Chest-
nut Hill, Mass.: Boston College, 1999.
Panel Study of Income Dynamics. Institute for Social Research, University of
Michigan, 2001. [http://psidonline.isr.umich.edu/].
Rosenberg, C. N. *Wealthy and Wise: How You and America Can Get the Most
Out of Your Giving.* New York: Little, Brown, 1994.
Steinberg, R., and Wilhelm, M. "Patterns of Giving and Volunteering in
COPPS 2001" (working paper). Indianapolis: IUPUI Department of Eco-
nomics, 2003.
Steinberg, R., Wilhelm, M., Brown, E., and Rooney, P. "Inheritance and
Charitable Donations" (working paper). Indianapolis: IUPUI Department
of Economics, 2003.
Wilhelm, M. "The Distribution of Giving in Six Surveys" (working paper).
Indianapolis: IUPUI Department of Economics, 2003.
Wilhelm, M., Brown, E., Rooney, P., and Steinberg, R. 2003. "The Inter-
generational Transmission of Generosity" (working paper). Indianapolis:
IUPUI Department of Economics, 2003.

RICHARD STEINBERG *is a professor of economics, philanthropic studies,
and public affairs and also associate director of the Center on Philanthropy
Panel Study (COPPS) at Indiana University Purdue University Indianapolis (IUPUI).*

MARK WILHELM *is associate professor of economics and philanthropic studies and director of COPPS at Indiana University Purdue University
Indianapolis.*

Development professionals exist in the gap between their institutions and their missions and benefactors and their values systems, providing a vital connection. Along with their benefactors, they too can be transformed in the development process and become more and more human through living well-examined lives.

7

Transforming philanthropy: Generativity, philanthropy, and the reflective practitioner

James M. Hodge

CAN A PHILANTHROPIC IMPULSE or proclivity be transmitted from one generation to the next? Can parents and mentors model philanthropic behaviors that are culturally contagious? How wonderful to ponder such ideas in theory and to consider that we humans might well be both hardwired and software-compatible for philanthropic tendencies. More and more evolutionary biologists are exploring humankind's innate potential for fairness and sharing behaviors (Wade, 2003).

As intriguing and enchanting as these theories are, the work that awaits us as practitioners each Monday morning reminds us that we need to bridge the chasm between theory and practice rapidly and cast a pragmatic eye on the plethora of philanthropic theory. Keeping both the big picture and that little pragmatic voice in balance

NEW DIRECTIONS FOR PHILANTHROPIC FUNDRAISING, NO. 42, WINTER 2003 © WILEY PERIODICALS, INC.

requires the enlightened practitioner to sift through reams of theory and then apply the "best" to daily practice and put the "rest" aside for further reflection. For we must engage both our left and right brains—our cognitive and affective sides—to be effective professionals. We must determine what can be learned from educators, psychologists, social biologists, and philosophers the likes of Paul Schervish, Erik Erikson, Michael O'Neill, Martin Buber, and Viktor Frankl, to name a few. And as Viktor Frankl reminds us, "It is not a matter of technique per se, but rather the spirit behind the technique that is important" (Frankl, 1984, p. 29). Too often, development officers and consultants focus on fundraising techniques rather than on the spirit of philanthropy, particularly in the education of newcomers to our profession. Hence, there is a need to transform ourselves and our work.

Three stages of philanthropic giving

I contend that there are three stages of philanthropic giving: transactional, transitional, and transformational. Transactional philanthropy is the regular "give-and-take" of our work: we ask and donors give, without much reflection on the part of either. It might even be seen as a zero-sum game. We get, they give, we become more, and they become less. In the world of transactions, development officers seek the gift.

In transitional philanthropy, donors develop more "relationship equity" with a nonprofit organization, usually through volunteering and making more and larger gifts. The focus, however, remains on the institution, its mission, and its vision for the future—its need for philanthropy.

In transformational philanthropy, donors meaningfully share of themselves and their assets. This is the world of donor-centric philanthropy, of Schervish's discernment or inclination model of philanthropy, rather than of a shaming model (Schervish, 2000).

In transactional philanthropy donors are pushed to give. Transitional philanthropy involves both push and pull. But in transformational philanthropy there is a compelling vision created by the organization and shared by the development officer that draws or attracts benefactors and their giving.

With transactional philanthropy we seek gifts (nouns). In transitional philanthropy, we seek campaign or capital, mega or ultimate gifts (adjectives). But in transformational philanthropy, we celebrate giving. Gift becomes a verb. Development officers walk with benefactors to find meaning through acts of philanthropy.

I contend that adults—through their ages, stages, and significant emotional events—can find meaning through philanthropy in much the same way that many seek meaning in their lives through churches and mosques, temples and shrines. Transformational philanthropy becomes more the pull of philanthropy than the push of philanthropy. Simply put, as professionals we must stop chasing money and start pursuing meaning in philanthropy.

Eight stages of adult development

With that context, let us strap on metaphoric seat belts and roar through some two hundred thousand years of human development, seeking important intersections between the theory and practice of philanthropy as it relates to generativity. Editorial limits allow only a *Cliff's Notes* version of Erik Erikson's final stages of adult development and what in the world that might have to do with the daily work of development practitioners. Interestingly, Erikson's original eight stages of development were extended and enhanced after his death by his wife, Joan Erikson, who was at the time in her eighties.

Let us look particularly at his last stages. The reason for focusing on the final life stages should be self-evident. Development officers must consider in what decade or decades donors make gifts of significance to nonprofit organizations. Anecdotal studies conducted at the Mayo Clinic and other health care nonprofits have found that significant gifts are most often made when donors are in their early seventies through their eighties and beyond.

An author once described the stages of a woman's life as twenty years of learning, twenty years of earning, and twenty years of returning, to which Dr. Joan Erikson no doubt would have added,

"Twenty years of discerning!" If this is true for both men and women, then perhaps it is in one's later years that truly significant gifts are contemplated and committed. Perhaps there is a correlation between Erikson's studies of generativity and acts of philanthropy. Erikson told us that as children, our primary psychological focus is on the self and receiving from others; in our twenties the focus is on mate selection, again primarily to satisfy our own needs; in our thirties and forties the focus shifts to raising children and advancing our careers; and in our fifties and sixties there is perhaps a focus on grandchildren. But when people are in their seventies and eighties and older, psychological roles are less clear compared with earlier ages, and they are challenged to make a shift to generativity and integrity—giving back to others beyond the family, and in fact, to the environment and to the world. This is when Erikson's challenge occurs, and perhaps when the greatest opportunities present themselves to development professionals and benefactors alike. One can either take this step toward generativity . . . and grow *out into* the world (generativity) or *turn into* oneself (stagnation); one can either give to the world or stagnate. Generativity or stagnation. We can either make our lives a gift, or we can become self-absorbed. We can become philanthropists, or we can become "stackers of cordwood," those sad souls whose only wish is to guard their accumulated assets or obsess about their personal safety. Practitioners of considerable experience have deduced that if safety and security are life's principal focus and purpose . . . individuals will never have enough money, nor ever be safe enough.

According to Erikson, one of the final tasks in life is to reach integrity. Integrity, as he defined it, is the "spiritual response to the intimations of the holy, the powerful, and the messages of earth and of the heavens" (Erikson and Erikson, 1997, p. 8). "Integrity has the function of promoting contact with the world, with things, and above all, with people; it is a tactile and tangible way to live, not an intangible goal to seek and to achieve" (p. 9). Generativity and integrity are most often achieved later in life, when one is seventy or eighty years old. Erikson remarked, "There is something one might call indomitable about many old people" (p. 9). He called it an "invariable core, the existential identity, that is, the integration of past, present, and future; it transcends the self and underscores the presence of intergenerational links" (p. 9). This is the essence of the eighth stage of life.

Other researchers have postulated similar theories to those of Erikson. Sober and Wilson, in their fascinating book *Unto Others: The Evolution and Psychology of Unselfish Behavior* (1998), noted, "Perhaps people care about others for hedonistic reasons early in life, but then their desires change—they come to care about others as ends in themselves" (p. 222). Similarly, Emmons in his text *The Psychology of Ultimate Concerns* says, "Embedding one's finite life with a grander and all-encompassing narrative appears to be a universal need" (p. 5). Continuing, Emmons tells us, "When other avenues fail to bring ultimate fulfillment, spiritual concerns rise in the value hierarchy in people's quests for a satisfying quality of life. People need meaning to survive; religion provides a powerful source of meaning" (1999, pp. 9–10). I contend that philanthropy does as well.

Lars Tornstom in his view of adult development believed that in later stages of life individuals can undergo "gerotranscendence," which he defined as a "shift in meta-perspective from a materialistic and rational vision to a more cosmic and transcendent one, normally followed by an increase in life satisfaction" (quoted in Erikson and Erikson, 1997, p. 123). Joan Erikson put it this way: "In truth we are called to become more and more human; we must discover the freedom to go beyond limits imposed on us by our world and seek fulfillment." She continued, "In the beginning we are what we are given; by midlife, when we have finally learned to stand on our own two feet, we learn that to complete our lives, we are called to give to others so that when we leave this world, we can be what we have given" (Erikson and Erikson, 1997, p. 126). Paul Schervish expresses a similar sentiment when he describes our work as "helping donors to excavate their biographical history, or moral biography, their contemporary prospects and purposes, and their anxieties and aspirations for the future" (Schervish, 2000, p. 25). Donors and development officers alike are compelled to complete their lives and philanthropy plays a starring role in helping both to do so. For philanthropic practitioners, that is something worth pondering on a busy Monday morning!

Generativity or stagnation. Giving out unto the world or giving in to self-absorption. Giving until it feels good . . . sometimes through the "hurt," where philanthropy is chosen above other values in a hierarchy. This idea transforms everything we do. Michael O'Neill observed that "the relatively new profession of development has added to the societal pool of moral trainers" (O'Neill, 1993, p. 30). Development officers have the potential to conduct themselves as moral trainers. But we cannot give benefactors "our" answers to the meaning of life through philanthropy, for as moral trainers we are, in fact, freed from "having all the answers." However, we are compelled to know the "master key" questions and to be in meaningful dialogue with donors. Through inquiring and inspiring, we can gently stretch and challenge donors to find meaning in life, often through the missions and visions of our nonprofit organizations.

Development officers are *not* in the manipulative business of "bottling home" and selling it back to benefactors—that is, cleverly finding, as one benefactor put it, "donors' buttons and hooks." As Paul Schervish advises us, we should "not give our moral compass to others." We *are* in the business of helping donors to explore their values systems and asking them to consider thoughts they have never had, nor might ever have dreamed of, had we not come into their lives. For development professionals simply do not sell widgets; instead, they promote wizards and wonders. Benefactors are not less having come to know the best of us, they are more. They live more well-examined lives because of the important dialogues we have with them.

Deathbed thinking: The ultimate test of generativity

What is the ultimate test of generativity? Perhaps it can be found in deathbed thinking. Could exploring what people contemplate on their deathbeds tell us about what, in retrospect, most truly value? How can knowing deathbed concerns help us shape values-clarifying questions? In rereading Kubler-Ross's *On Death and Dying* (1997), exploring writings from the hospice movement, and interviewing hospice workers, I discovered startling similarities in people's thoughts in the final days and weeks of their lives. On their deathbeds individuals were not saying, "I am worth $1.8 million and that has brought meaning to my life." Instead three recurring questions seem to be on their minds. What was the meaning of my life? (Not what is the meaning of life.) Did I make a difference in the world? And, finally, what is my legacy in the world? In other words, they are thinking about making a difference and leaving a legacy. . . . Does that sound vaguely familiar? As moral trainers, we development professionals are compelled to remember this deathbed thinking and to consider our role in *helping people to arrive before they depart!*

This idea no doubt causes pragmatic and technique-driven fundraisers to gnash their teeth and cry out, "How does this apply to me as a practitioner?" First, our profession must make a trans-formational shift from fundraising to moral training, to believing in the noble role of philanthropy and its transformative power in peoples' lives. Second, development officers must consider what master key questions help people lead well-examined lives. These are questions focused on meaning and making a difference, on leaving a legacy and how donors can be remembered for a life of giving back to the world. This is the arena of values-based inquiry and ethical inspiration and generativity.

For two hundred thousand years, for ten thousand generations, humankind existed as hunter-gatherers. And although Darwin suggested that on an individual basis the survival of the fittest reigns supreme, on a group level those societies that are more caring and sharing than other groups actually have more offspring and flourish more than groups of people who are all out for their own selfish needs. Emmons agreed, asserting, "The idea that individuals exist to benefit their society may be more common than the idea that society is merely a collection of selfish individuals" (1999, p. 10). Thus, perhaps humans are hardwired for altruistic acts.

Four basic human drives

Philanthropists or cordwood stackers? How do these tendencies develop? One explanation might come from an intriguing book called *Driven: How Human Nature Shapes Our Choices* by Paul R. Lawrence and Nitin Nohria of Harvard University (2002). Lawrence and Nohria contend that humans have four basic drives. Times allows only the briefest review of this work. The authors posit these four universal characteristics are those which make us human. They are biological drives that motivate us as human beings. This work explores the latest findings from evolutionary biology and thoughts about human behavior from the social scientists.

The way we act is a result of conscious decisions we all make, but the authors believe there are constant struggles between the four innate, subconscious brain-based drives. The drives are (in my order, not the authors'):

- The drive to acquire objects and experiences that improve our status relative to others
- The drive to defend ourselves, our loved ones, our beliefs, and our resources from harm
- The drive to learn and make sense of the world and of ourselves
- The drive to bond with others in long-term relationships of mutual care and concern

Lawrence and Nohria contend that humans will always be contentious and never reach the ideal balance among the four drives. They believe, however, that if individuals attempt to balance these drives they can find a way forward to the next stage of human evolution.

Neglected, the drive to acquire can make a person envious and lack self-esteem. Neglecting to bond can leave a person empty and disconnected. Neglecting to learn can lead to a life with few opportunities to pursue passions and curiosities and leave one stunted. Neglecting the drive to defend can leave a person vulnerable.

Perhaps those who become stuck in the drives to acquire and defend wind up with the "cordwood stacking" syndrome—hoarding. In contrast, those souls whose drives to learn and bond are strong may more readily transform into philanthropists.

What it all means for development professionals

Perhaps development professionals need to consider how to recognize these drives and encourage individuals through inquiry to grow in all four dimensions. Generativity certainly requires a strong need to bond and to share and to care for others and the world.

Perhaps by identifying benefactors in our midst who have well-cultivated drives to learn and bond, we may find receptivity to meaningful dialogues that are more likely to foster philanthropic actions. Perhaps planned-giving professionals can walk for a while with those more inclined to acquiring and defending—the cordwood stackers—and hope for some ultimate sharing through estate-planning processes.

Perhaps we are not only hardwired and driven for philanthropy, but software-compatible as well. Erikson and other developmental psychologists, through their theories of the stages of development, may be saying that humans grow, develop, and eventually mature toward generativity through acts of kindness and giving of themselves to others.

Taking this stance means clearing the brush from Robert Frost's *road less traveled* and returning to our ancestral roots, to those days when humans lived in extended family groups. It is about returning to the campfires where our parents and grandparents lived out their values, their personal strivings, and their ever-deepening needs to care . . . right in front of the eyes of the generations who followed. Consider how in times past the cycle of life was more apparent as children moved from "being cared for" to adults who "took care of" to grandparents who "cared for the earth we all inhabit." Our ancestors had role and soul models sharing the same huts and hovels. They not only cared for their families but cared for each other. Eventually, they cared for others outside their social circles. This is the long feedback loop, or what Robert Payton (1988) called *serial reciprocity*. Kittredge exclaims that "altruism is generosity to strangers and ways of life we never expect to encounter as a method of preserving both biological and cultural multiplicity and possibility. Acting generously helps many of us feel increasingly purposeful and coherent" (Kittredge, 2001, p. 34). Rituals, dances, songs, and oral history made maps for those who followed. Somehow, reality TV seems a poor substitute for the transmission of family values.

As moral trainers, development officers must acknowledge the power of oral traditions and tell instructive stories of transformative benefaction and inspiring benefactors. "We need stories that encourage us to think that being good is giving nourishment and taking all possible responsibility" (Kittredge, 2001, p. 253). Those in health care nonprofits must tell stories and become moral mentors, illustrating the moral imperative that we and our philanthropic partners have to cure disease, to palliate pain, to offer hope. Better yet, we must encourage donors to tell their stories so that others naturally exclaim, "I could do that as well!" Singer and Salovey contend that "the stories individuals tell us about their own life is the lifeblood of personality" (cited in Emmons, 1999, p. 70). Asking opinions, telling stories of the impact of philanthropy on the lives we serve, making a difference, *seeding values*, leaving a legacy: fundraisers thus become like ancient cartographers drawing maps for benefactors and encouraging them to lead well-examined philanthropical lives. With this as context, professionals should visit cherished champions of their organization, break bread with them, gather around their *campfire*, and talk the stuff of shared values.

To accomplish this transformation in our work, we must be alert to significant emotional events and "triggers" in the lives of benefactors, a shift in Eriksonian stages. Development professionals need to be aware of triggers and shifts and how through ethical inquiry they can help benefactors achieve generativity in thought and deed. As moral trainers, development officers must consider important questions that might encourage adult development.

What are some of the most poignant master key questions? They are questions that explore core family values, discover role models in the lives of benefactors, and delve into donors' most meaningful experiences in philanthropy. Such questions inform the development officer about important people, organizations, and experiences in a philanthropist's life. They are questions that help us understand how individuals and families make decisions and what donors' learning and social styles are. They create provocative, engaging, and compelling proposals for partnerships. Exploring with individuals their sense of the social responsibility of wealth and how family values can be perpetuated through philanthropy allows them to see critical overlaps between their personal values and institutional missions.

The overlap between donor values and institutional mission is where the "dance of philanthropy" happens. We ask the donor, "What is the project of your life?" "What really matters to you?" "When someone speaks your name, what thought, what idea, what grand plan will come to mind?" We must inquire, "What is it you are striving for?" "What is your passion?" Klinger exclaims, "Goal striving is a fundamental feature of living organisms. Human brains in particular are wired for purposeful living and life itself is a continuous stream of goal pursuits" (cited in Emmons, 1999, p. 48). "Generational strivings are defined as those strivings that involve creating, giving of oneself to others, and having an influence on future generations" (cited in Emmons, 1999, p. 48). All questions that explore the meaning of benefactors' lives, how they see their life work making a positive difference in the world, and how through careful planning they can leave a lasting monument to the world, help them answer the proverbial deathbed questions.

It is often the case that one can learn more about donors' motivational makeup, their personal strivings, and their life projects through inquiry about their avocations (their passions) than about their vocations (their work). Of course, there are many times, particularly with entrepreneurs, when their passion is their work.

By learning about people's passions we may discover how a "passion graft"—an organization's passion and vision—might adhere to a donor's value system. And in some great moments, a benefactor's previous passion, for his business perhaps, gives way to a full-fledged "passion transplant" to an organizational vision and mission. It has also been a wonderful thing to witness a benefactor's passion turning to compassion as heath care nonprofits strive to understand better the nature and causes of disease, to relieve the next generation's pain and suffering.

There is a taxonomy of questions to consider as we engage donors, from inquiries about the facts of their lives to evaluative questions about strongly held values and beliefs. A requisite amount of relationship or social equity must exist before we can ask highly personal questions of value. It is important to recognize when, in our developing relationships, and in their stages of life, it is permissible to ask questions of significance. Development officers must seek permission to ask these questions and concurrently guarantee protections that dialogues will be safe and confidential.

However, the process of inquiry, centered on values, is, as previously stated, more about the spirit of the interactions and engagements than about taxonomies, matrixes, and questioning techniques. Bill Sturtevant (1997, 2001) is often referenced as saying that major gifts are "stop-and-think gifts." I contend that transformational gifts are "stop, think, and feel gifts." Composing questions of significance requires more art than science, is more right- than left-brained, is about feeling rather than mere cognition. This may frighten male development officers, and perhaps with good reason, for transformational philanthropy is a whole lot closer in spirit to communal gathering than to hunting. Perhaps future workshops will assist those of us who are male and "affectively challenged" to get in touch with our right brains and encourage us to seek out female mentors and discover how our female colleagues use both their left and their right brains for philanthropy.

If we do all this, we will enter with our donors into "I-thou" relationships, which the great German philosopher Martin Buber (1970) has encouraged, the state of grace where we view donors and their personal development as an end in itself. We do not see donors as a means to an end, the mere transaction of moving money from their pockets to ours. We stop chasing money and start pursuing meaning. For to paraphrase Tom Morris in his profound and delightful book *If Aristotle Ran General Motors*, "If we put people first and projects second [in our case, gifts], if you have good relations with people, the gifts will come. And if you focus more on the people than the gifts, the gifts will tend to go far beyond what you might otherwise expect" (Morris, 1997, p. 24).

We are all weary of being manipulated politically for our votes, economically for our consumerism, and philanthropically for our gifts. There are at least three reasons, in addition to the obvious ethical considerations, why it is not smart to manipulate benefactors: first, because benefactors are smarter than we are. Second, because benefactors know how to make money. And third, and most importantly, because benefactors have witnessed every possible scheme to relieve them of their money! Therefore, we must *stop scheming and start dreaming* with our benefactors.

What do we owe transformational benefactors? Quite simply we owe them a full accounting, through stewardship, of the meaning behind their gifts and the difference those gifts make. As Kay Sprinkel Grace has suggested in her book *High Impact Philanthropy* (Grace and Wendroff, 2001), we must always demonstrate the impact philanthropy has on the real lives of those we serve.

Stewardship is not only a moral obligation, the right thing to do, but also the smart thing to do. Donors report that stewardship links them back to the good feelings evoked when they first committed to a gift. Stewardship begets great philanthropic commitments.

Stewardship requires us whenever we are with donors, board members, and volunteers to tell "isn't-it-amazing" stories of how our organizations make both tangible and intangible differences in peoples' lives. Our benefactors do not need more plaques in return for their gifts. In fact, many years ago a benefactor admonished me, "Please don't send me another marble paperweight for my gift. . . . I have enough now to build my mausoleum!" Instead of "trinkets," we should be giving "think-its" of how the world is better because of their philanthropy.

In a talk given many years ago, Sheldon Garber (1993) likened development officers to "agents of change" in our organizations and the lives of benefactors. As agents of change, development officers are called to help cast the organizational vision, shape the nonprofit mission, engage donors in important dialogues, be moral trainers, and change lives. This work we do is far more a calling than an occupation. This stance toward our work is poignantly illustrated by Robert Payton's probing question, "Do you live for philanthropy or do you live off of philanthropy?" (Payton, 1988, p. 71).

With apologies to both God and Michelangelo, development professionals exist in the gap, the gap between the institution and its mission and the benefactor and his or her values systems. This gap is similar to that portrayed by Michelangelo on the ceiling of the Sistine Chapel. We exist to provide a vital connection between benefactors and our institutions. We have the delicious challenge of exploring the intersections between donor values and institutional missions. We act as conductors both literally and figuratively, as in conductors of electricity and conductors who orchestrate philanthropy. We are compelled to sing to the source of the spring, to help pass each other along on our journeys, *to become*, as Jonas Salk once put it, *good ancestors*. We, along with our benefactors, will be transformed in the process and become more and more human through living well-examined lives.

Transactions, transitions, and transformations. We have a choice. We can be like Garber's shepherds, who tend their flocks in lower fields, count their sheep, and conduct that old *grass-for-meat-and-wool* transaction. Or we can be like Sherpas, who guide donors up the institutions' mountains and seek gifts for our institutions' needs and missions. Or ultimately, we can be like shamans, who walk with donors up virtual mountains that we create together.

We are all both forward-leaning and forward-thinking beings, and as such our souls require spiritual points along the horizon on which to fix our eyes. We must therefore share good visions. We are called to go beyond limits imposed on us by our often "needy" and materialistic institutions to find the deeper well of meaning and its partner, fulfillment. If we do, benefactors will be compelled to walk with us on mutual vision quests, through generativity and philanthropy, to integrity. And if we celebrate these partners and the partnerships rather than their financial assets, we will walk on the supply side of philanthropy that Paul Schervish assures us is out there. And we shall be rich in benefaction both material and spiritual.

References

Buber, M. *I and Thou.* New York: Scribner's, 1970.

Collier, C. W. *Wealth in Families.* Cambridge, Mass.: Harvard University Press, 2001.

Emmons, R. A. *The Psychology of Ultimate Concerns: Motivation and Spirituality in Personality.* New York: Guilford Press, 1999.

Erikson, E. H., and Erikson, J. M. *The Life Cycle Completed.* New York: W. W. Norton, 1997.

Frankl, V. E. *Man's Search for Meaning: An Introduction to Logotherapy.* New York: Simon & Schuster, 1984.

Garber, S. "The Fund Raising Professional: An Agent for Change." Paper presented to the International Conference for the Association of Healthcare Philanthropy, Chicago, Oct. 4, 1993.

Grace, K. S., and Wendroff, A. L. *High Impact Philanthropy.* New York: Wiley, 2001.

Kittredge, W. *The Nature of Generosity.* New York: Vintage Books, 2001.

Kubler-Ross, E. *On Death and Dying.* New York: Scribner's, 1997.

Lawrence, P. R., and Nohria, N. *Driven: How Human Nature Shapes Our Choices.* San Francisco: Jossey-Bass, 2002.

Morris, T. *If Aristotle Ran General Motors.* Austin, Tex.: Holt, Rinehart and Winston, 1997.

O'Neill, M. "Fund Raising As an Ethical Act." Advancing Philanthropy, National Society of Fund Raising Executives, Fall 1993 (*1*), 30–35.

Payton, R. L. *Philanthropy: Voluntary Action for the Public Good.* New York: American Council on Education, 1988.

Schervish, P. G. "The Material Horizons of Philanthropy: New Directions for Money and Motives." In E. R. Tempel and D. F. Burlingame (eds.), *Understanding the Needs of Donors: The Supply Side of Charitable Giving.* New Directions in Philanthropic Fundraising, no. 29. San Francisco: Jossey-Bass, 2000, 17–31.

Sober, E., and Wilson, D. S. *Unto Others: The Evolution and Psychology of Unselfish Behavior.* Cambridge, Mass.: Harvard University Press, 1998.

Sturtevant, W. T. *The Artful Journey: Cultivating and Soliciting the Major Gifts.* Chicago: Bonus Books, Inc., 1997.

Sturtevant, W. T. *The Continuing Journey: Stewardship and Useful Case Studies in Philanthropy.* Chicago: Bonus Books, Inc., 2001.

Wade, N. "Play Fair: Your Life May Depend on It." *New York Times,* Sept. 21, 2003, Section 4, p. 12.

JAMES M. HODGE *is a manager of the Principal Gifts Program at Mayo Clinic in Rochester, Minnesota.*

As new donors approach philanthropy, many look first to define their work and then to which vehicle they might use to accomplish it. Also, many are making more collaborative efforts to address complex social issues. In this chapter, the former board chair of the Foundation Incubator discusses addressing the needs of this emerging audience.

8

Leadership in emerging family philanthropy

Lorna M. Lathram

THE LAST FIVE YEARS have brought considerable growth, development, and transition to philanthropy, with one of the largest increases being in the number of new family foundations. At the same time, a new style of organization and leadership is developing, reflecting today's new donors.

My experience has been in working with new and emerging organizations during this period of growth and transition, initially as founding executive director of a new family foundation in Silicon Valley, most recently as board chair of the Foundation Incubator in Palo Alto. This organization is dedicated to stimulating innovation and collaboration in philanthropy.

The purpose of this chapter is to discuss leadership in emerging family philanthropies. First, however, it is important to look at the context: the current field of philanthropy. What does the field look

NEW DIRECTIONS FOR PHILANTHROPIC FUNDRAISING, NO. 42, WINTER 2003 © WILEY PERIODICALS, INC.

like? What does *emerging* philanthropy look like? What is leadership's role?

Philanthropy today: Changing people and practices

The social sector has demonstrated unprecedented growth in the last twenty-five years. Even with the current economic downturn, growth is expected to continue over the next decade. U.S. giving reached nearly $241 billion in 2002 and is projected to reach $300 billion by 2012. Currently, giving by individuals accounts for almost 80 percent of all donations (*Giving USA 2003*, 2003). Giving by foundations accounts for approximately $27 billion, or about 11 percent of all donations. There are over sixty thousand U.S. foundations, nearly double the number of organizations and triple the amount of giving of the previous decade (Foundation Center, 2003). Furthermore, continued foundation growth is projected, with the number expected to reach one hundred thousand by 2010.

Private or family foundations, currently numbering forty thousand, are only one form of organized philanthropy. Forty-two new community foundations were created in 2001, with an 11 percent increase in giving that year by community foundations, allowing donors another vehicle through which to accomplish their philanthropy (Foundation Center, 2003).

Employing a multiplicity of giving vehicles

New entrants into philanthropy are diversifying their giving vehicles just as they have diversified their portfolios. Besides foundations, various other forms of philanthropic giving are in place to serve their needs and desires, including donor advised funds (DAFs) and giving circles. By using a multiplicity of vehicles and employing the appropriate "tool" for the job, donors can achieve the right mix of control and flexibility.

As these new donors approach philanthropy, many look first to define their work and then to which vehicle to use to accomplish

Figure 8.1. Philanthropic giving vehicles

Gift of cash to charity	Giving circle	Donor advised fund	Supporting organization	Private foundation	Split interest trust or charitable remainder trust

flexibility/control →

it. This is a different way of thinking; it allows the exploration of alternative vehicles. Many options cost less and provide greater flexibility than forming a foundation. They may also be used in conjunction with foundations, because they are not mutually exclusive. The new vehicles often offer the opportunity for greater control, personal engagement, and experiential learning.

For example, if a donor already has a family foundation dedicated to domestic work but desires to do international funding, she may choose a donor advised fund. Such funds are also well suited for donors who wish to fund locally when their foundation has a national focus. They are appropriate too if the donors wish to fund issues or initiatives not strategically aligned with their foundation, or perhaps, to make an anonymous gift. Donors may have multiple DAFs, each with its own purpose.

Figure 8.1 illustrates the range of vehicles available to philanthropists today.

Making collaborative efforts

Although they often work in isolation, philanthropists and philanthropies today are making more collaborative efforts to address complex social issues. The organizations' founders, who often discovered great value in collaborations, partnerships, and strategic alliances in their previous careers, are driving much of this movement.

Affiliates of the Foundation Incubator have the option of participating in a funding collaborative. This type of funding requires a different skill set: learning to work closely with partners across organizational lines. Although the intent and the missions may be aligned, other important issues must be considered, such as style, operations, and most key, organizational culture. When contemplating funding collaboratives, the cost of the human investment must be considered too.

Bridging skills and blurring worlds

The number of young philanthropists coming from the private sector is influencing the models and movements in emerging philanthropy, because they bring with them an entrepreneurial style and spirit. Old models are being challenged, best practices from the business world are being applied and modified, and new alliances are being struck.

"Social entrepreneurship" and "engaged philanthropy" are products of this new thinking. Such models give new philanthropists the opportunity to take a more hands-on approach, engage with others entering the field, and practice, experiment, and learn. These philanthropists bring their ideas, business experience, time, and networks. Applying the culture and expertise they gained through their experience in business, they network with others in the field, leveraging their collective skills, time, funds, and resources to invest more effectively in social change. These philanthropists actively seek ways to work together more efficiently and effectively in order to maximize the return on their individual investments.

New donors and philanthropies are also leveraging technology, especially the Internet, to reach a larger audience and facilitate collaboration in order to determine and use resources most effectively.

Aidmatrix, created by the i2 Foundation, is an excellent example of the use of technology. Aidmatrix is an Internet-based solution that facilitates the exchange of humanitarian goods between suppliers and organizations that serve people in need. During its first year in existence, Aidmatrix helped meet the needs of over 3.6 million people by delivering more than 29 million meals and 36 million pounds of food.

The Aidmatrix concept was born at i2, which recognized that its supply chain management solutions could significantly improve the connection between humanitarian aid organizations and parties who want to make donations. The i2 Foundation, formed by i2 employees, launched Aidmatrix in October 2000. With i2 as a founding partner, other vendors of the complementary technologies necessary to bring Aidmatrix to fruition were approached to form a collaborative effort.

In its first year of existence, Aidmatrix changed the way charitable donations were made. In the past, nonprofit agencies such as homeless shelters, soup kitchens, and children's after-school programs did not consistently receive the goods they ordered from food banks because they had no visibility into the actual inventory available at any given time. Today, food banks using Aidmatrix dramatically increase their ability to fill orders to these agencies, which can order around the clock from inventory. The result is better ability to allocate high-demand items across the entire food bank community, faster turnaround on orders, and greater trust between the food banks and their agencies. Food banks can increase the number of agencies they serve while at the same time reducing the time that products sit in scarce and costly warehouse space.

Extending the leadership role

As they did in their business careers, many of the new philanthropists are recognizing the value and importance of extending the leadership role beyond organizational boundaries of their particular philanthropic interest. They recognize that it is critical to provide time and energy to build the whole field of philanthropy. This is not a new concept, but it is one not widely practiced in organized philanthropy. Field, or capacity building, has traditionally been for nonprofit organizations, but many now believe it extends to the philanthropic side. They believe that funding organizations like the Center on Philanthropy at Indiana University or the Foundation Incubator are vital to the growth and development of philanthropy as a field.

Field or capacity building provides the operational undergirding of the new philanthropists' organizations and the work they do. It affects their partners, alliances, funding projects, and even the structure of their boards, because it is not just a philosophy but also a practice. Founders, staff, and board must be ready to commit time, expertise, and funding to build the field and infrastructure of philanthropy.

A look at the emerging stage of new philanthropies

The emerging stage of a philanthropic organization is complex and varies depending on a host of factors, including the experience of the participants, their approach to philanthropy (which, as already noted, is often influenced by their business experience), their available resources, and the stage or depth of articulation of the founder's philanthropic desires. The emerging stage is different for every organization, but generally it lasts from two to five years. Although the time frame may differ, organizations in this stage go through common phases of development.

Discovery

During the discovery phase, the organization researches and gathers information, learns about the field, makes connections, builds networks, and develops a personal philanthropic philosophy and desired area of work. A general vision, mission, and purpose are often developed during this phase.

Building and planning

Greater internal development occurs during the building and planning phase. There is a deeper level of research and understanding of the philanthropic issues, the field, and personal motivations. The desired philanthropic vehicles are chosen and the organization's infrastructure is built. The mission and vision are refined, and planning begins: strategic, business, and financial. A more extensive search for targeted information and expertise to support further development is in progress.

At the Foundation Incubator, we found that organizations were looking for focused information that provided specific answers and models for their development. Resources include access to established organizations and leaders, advisers, and consultants, peer-to-peer networking, and other support services. As the organization sets its course, networking and customized feedback become increasingly important.

We have found that the key areas in which information is sought are the "art and craft" of grant making, focus or issue areas, capacity building, board development, technical assistance, collaborations, evaluations, sector trends, advocacy work, international funding, organizational effectiveness, and community building. Having the right information accelerates the developmental process and helps combat feelings of isolation that are common at this stage.

Experimentation and practice

Once the decision makers have gathered and processed the information, they need to begin applying and testing their ideas. At this point, many new to philanthropy experiment, building on their areas of expertise, looking to implement innovative ideas and approaches. Grants are made. The focus is still largely internal, but the organization has started practicing the art of philanthropy and developing its expertise. Evaluative measures and methods are considered to address the age-old question: *How will we know if our work has brought value and positive results?* This is often difficult because, unlike in the private sector, there is no immediate feedback loop. Foundations must have the ability to "stick to it."

Considerations in the leadership role of advising new philanthropists

Addressing the needs of this audience is complex, requiring customized and timely attention from staff. To assimilate a new venture in a family structure, it is necessary for staff to match individual needs with the varied experience of family members, mesh the desires of the "whole" with the various interests of the individuals involved, and provide sector education in conjunction with building an organization.

Significant wealth has a shorter gestation period

With the immense growth of technology-based industries, it no longer takes a lifetime or even decades to amass significant wealth; it sometimes happens in only a few years. Many new philanthropists feel they have an opportunity and a responsibility to provide resources and guidance to enable social change, and they carefully design and implement giving in ways that best meet the "market" needs while also aligning with their personal goals and values. Often, young philanthropists are not as concerned with their legacy as they are about doing the work, directly influencing the organization or the giving approach.

Leadership works best in partnership with the family

One of the greatest differences between an emerging philanthropy and an established one is that the philanthropists themselves are often engaged, involved—and alive! Those in an advisory leadership role have the opportunity to work with people who are making a life change to a new role—a new direction. It is their *new* work, often based on the philosophy attributed to Winston Churchill: "We make a living by what we get, we make a life by what we give."

This is very personal and intimate work. It is crucial to build trust with the philanthropists and their families. Early advisers are often legal and financial; they may even be on the boards of young organizations. Although leadership is needed both operationally and philosophically, developing the philosophical side of the organization and the individuals involved is the primary need at this stage. Leaders need to share the learning and understanding of the "art and craft" of grant making, support and encourage the family and the philanthropists in their journey of discovery, help articulate their vision, and assist in bringing that vision to life.

Philanthropy straddles the generations

In this environment, often a couple does the work or creates a philanthropy, and this requires a balance of styles, needs, and desires. The work also often encompasses multiple generations, from the philanthropist's children to his parents. This offers early opportunities, from issues of succession to how the founders will guide their children on their philanthropic journey. One interesting twist for this "sandwich generation" of philanthropists is their role, if any, in guiding or assimilating their parents' philanthropy. In many instances, multiple foundations or other vehicles are created to operationalize the varied interests represented in a family so that all can accomplish their individual missions without "mission creep" or disagreement.

Just-in-time learning is needed

When working with emerging philanthropic organizations, it is necessary to provide the founders and board with information on demand: "just-in-time" learning in a format they can easily assimilate. Findings, research, and briefings are often put into the vernacular of business as the organization develops its own communication style.

We have found that many systems, or "tools," can be used to communicate the work and findings of an organization, including an organizational CD, a knowledge management system, Power-Point briefings, newsletters, frequent board meetings, and retreats. It is best to vary the tools and approaches, because it is necessary to appeal to a number of learning and communication styles and preferences. The common thread in today's organizations is the use of digital data. The Web and e-mail facilitate this, enabling information to follow the team as it grapples with busy schedules and "virtual" offices.

Conclusion

These organizations are young, in a stage of development and experimentation with continuous learning and improvement. This is an exciting and continuously changing-morphing period for the long-term structure and the goals and vision of these philanthropists.

It is also a time to meet market needs with new ideas and strategies while remaining sensitive to cultural differences. People and organizations have been at this a long time, and it is important to be cognizant of that fact and make full use of the assistance and guidance so generously offered by the field. New organizations should try to make only *new mistakes* and learn from them, sharing the experience with others so that the field moves forward at an accelerated pace.

In businesses today, we discuss "built to last" but seldom "built in perpetuity." This is an important consideration in building a philanthropy, and it is a different way of thinking. The capacity required to go the distance—for the organization, the mission, the work, and the field—must be considered. It is important to establish an environment and create experiences to support this, and to consider goals, evaluation measures, and approaches for the long term.

To summarize, both family members and their advisers in leadership roles in emerging family philanthropy should do the following:

• Consider what must be accomplished, then think of the multiple vehicles available and select accordingly.
• Support the organization's growth and development but also the capacity and professionalism of the field.
• Be entrepreneurial in nature while honoring the knowledge of others. Experiment, but do not discount the knowledge, history, and experience of the sector.
• Establish an environment that is proactive and collaborative in nature.
• Enjoy the excitement of being a work in progress: evolve, learn, and grow.

References

Foundation Center. *The Foundation Yearbook.* New York: Foundation Center, 2003.
Giving USA 2003. Indianapolis: American Association of Fundraising Council (AAFRC) Trust for Philanthropy, 2003.

LORNA M. LATHRAM *is an independent consultant in Alameda, California.*

Giving takes work, and it is at its best when it is part of an attitude of gratitude. We give philanthropically because we need help in adequately showing that gratitude.

9

Paved with good intentions

David H. Smith

I WANT TO MAKE four points in this short chapter. Giving is a good thing, but it is tangled in a thicket of moral problems. Good giving therefore takes work, and it is at its best when it is part of an attitude of gratitude.

Giving is good

I begin with the apparently obvious assertion that giving is a good thing. We honor people who give; we are grateful for gifts; institutions that have done remarkable amounts of good have been enabled by gifts. It seems perverse to be critical or cynical about a kind of behavior that has done so much for so many of us.

But there are profound arguments against a social stress on giving. A great deal of the social and political philosophy of the past four hundred years can be seen as a series of meditations on the theme that we can best respond to the inevitable neediness of human beings with a focus on justice. Justice is understood to be an alternative to generosity, and a superior alternative at that. The language of justice is the language of rights and claims, but gifts are

NEW DIRECTIONS FOR PHILANTHROPIC FUNDRAISING, NO. 42, WINTER 2003 © WILEY PERIODICALS, INC.

not the sort of thing that anyone has a right to. The reason that much moral philosophy has stressed justice is the high value we all place on self-respect. When my needs for education or health care are seen as things that I have a *right* to fulfill, then I do not have to plead or beg or feel inferior to others who find themselves in a less needy position. When we think in terms of justice we think of problems that might befall any of us, and we agree to use our resources to help ourselves and one another. The fact that we are all actually or potentially needy is made clear. In contrast, when we rely on *giving* to meet needs, we too easily assume that the world can be divided into those who are needy and those who are not.

I will not attempt a full response to this argument here; indeed, I think it makes an irrefutable claim—that justice is a fundamental virtue of social institutions. The harder issue is whether our acknowledgment of the importance of self-respect should lead us to jettison a stress on giving as one of the social values we treasure and hope to inculcate. I do not think we should despise giving.

To start with, the need for assistance is simply there. Six thousand people die from AIDS each day in Africa, and one need only read any day's newspaper to see a litany of natural or human disasters, the suffering caused by human indifference and ambition. Given the magnitude of human need in the world, it seems foolish to despise anything that might help out. Moreover, it is clear that resources are there to be tapped. Two-thirds of U.S. households contributed a total of $2.1 billion to help after the September 11, 2001 disaster. Paul Schervish and colleagues speak of an expected transfer of $14 trillion of funds from one generation to another within the next fifty years (Schervish and Havens, 1999). *Perhaps* in an ideal world money would be equitably redistributed, but it seems sensible to put some effort into a strategy that suggests to persons the magnitude of the responsibility they have inherited.

Moreover, justice is blind. The statue of Justice rising over many courthouses shows her blindfolded. And she is cold. Justice is impartial and impersonal. Those are important qualities in a system of allocation, but they are insufficient specifications for the moral requirement of helping each other out. This is clear to us in families. Justice in the family is important, but a family in which justice is the only value observed would be a caricature. Social life would be flat if justice were our only standard. We need wiggle room for love and for giving, for spontaneity and indeed partiality.

Giving is a much studied term and it means different things to different people. In our ordinary usage we think of gifts as spontaneous, a surprise, unnecessary. When I was a student at Yale Divinity School in the early 1960s my wife and I were penurious. One cold December night we stood in line outside Woolsey Hall hoping to buy balcony tickets for a recital by the great cellist Rostropovich. A large man wearing a huge coat and a Russian hat approached us, asked us if we hoped to buy tickets to the recital, and—when we said yes—gave us two—indeed two of the best seats I have ever had in a major hall. The man was Chaplin William Sloane Coffin. That remarkable act beautifully illustrates our usual concept of the gift. Completely unexpected by the recipient, completely voluntary and unnecessary by the giver. It is a romantic notion of gift, nurtured in an individualistic society.

In contrast to this stands a more classical concept of gift as a distinctive form of social relation, a relation insightfully studied by Marcel Maus, Lewis Hyde, and others. When they talk about gifts these writers are identifying a form of social exchange that contrasts with market exchanges. On these terms gift giving is obligatory, not optional. Gifts are transactions that knit a social group together; they establish personal relations, and not giving a gift can cause a major social rupture. We are all familiar with this form of giving as well as the more romantic and individualistic type. Failing to provide a gift for an anniversary, birthday, Christmas, or bar mitzvah is to default on an obligation, and providing such gifts is a very important component in sustaining the nongovernmental web of social relations that holds a society together.

Whatever the motivation, and however these acts may be best described, it seems clear that some people, some of the time, are strongly motivated to give—and that society is the better for it.

Giving is fraught with moral peril

I have already suggested why meeting social needs through giving raises hackles among some. If we do not let those worries dissuade us from stressing the importance of giving, there are still many serious problems to resolve. I will identify two.

Whose need is being met when I make a gift? I may think someone who lives in another neighborhood needs education; he may think he needs food. Conflicts between the vision of the donor and that of the recipient are recurrent in the world of organized giving. For example, on learning that the Red Cross had followed its usual practice and held back some of the money donated for assistance after the September 11 disaster, one of my oldest friends remarked, "I'll never give to the Red Cross again." Participation in that particular rescue effort there and then was essential to him. He did not want generally to be a helpful person, he wanted to do something to help with that particular tragedy. With the best will in the world, his need to be involved overwhelmed sober judgment about what was actually needed. I will argue later that there is nothing wrong with the giver acknowledging her or his neediness—to the contrary. But sorting out the differences between the donor's needs and vision and the real needs of the moment can be difficult.

More troublesome are those situations where a desire to control or correct masquerades as a desire to give or to help. The giver begins with a full outline of what the good life entails and wants to help the recipient to . . . live up to those specific standards. This is what one moral theologian called the philanthropy of patronage, rather than the philanthropy of humility. It is a desire to dominate, not to empower through love. C. S. Lewis captured the problem in his quotation of an imaginary epitaph:

Erected by her sorrowing brothers,
in memory of Martha Clay.
Here lies one who lived for others.
Now she has peace,
And so have they.

How can we get out of the trap where both sides think in terms of power imbalance, with those who are privileged and powerful on one side and those who are needy on the other? I think an important first step is for all, beginning with the giver, to acknowledge their own neediness and dependence. The acknowledgment of this indisputable fact on the part of the apparently strong and powerful is particularly important. No one is really a self-made person. Everyone has been the beneficiary of individual assistance and social structures that enabled even the most self-directed ascent. Moreover, our own powers of intellect and will are scarcely earned or designed. They are the products of genetics and the social lottery, of fate or the enabling grace of God. The giving of humility, reciprocal giving, is impossible without a sense of neediness. Authentic giving is only possible for people who have internalized the sense that they have been given to.

The sense of donor finitude and gratefulness must, in authentic giving, be coupled with a sense of respect for the identity and particularity of those whom the donor wants to help. A wonderful reality of the modern world is the recognition of the glorious diversity of the human family. And one need not look far afield. Our own children are anything but mirrors of their parents. They bring their own light to the world, and I thank God for that! In the film *Seabiscuit*, Red Pollard's boss does not want to let Red ride again after a terrible accident and injury. Red's friend and fellow jockey, George Wolfe, intercedes with the owner, saying it is "better to let a man break his leg than to break his heart." Paternalistic attacks on self-respect are patronizing and insulting. Respecting dignity is a necessary condition of morally worthy giving.

Giving takes work

Coming to see oneself as someone who can give, and respecting the particularity of recipients, are not easy tasks for individuals or organizations. As we reflect on the work that giving entails, it may be helpful to distinguish various kinds of giving.

Philanthropy is only one kind of giving. Mother Teresa was a saint, perhaps, but it strains our ordinary usage of the word to call her a *philanthropist*. She fits the definition—a lover of humankind—but not the connotations that *philanthropy* has when used in ordinary speech. At the other extreme, if I call myself a philanthropist after dropping $10 in the Salvation Army bucket at Christmastime, this can only be understood as an attempt at a joke. Rather, *philanthropy* connotes a kind of scale or magnitude that is in some way unusual. It makes a splash; it makes a noticeable difference. Moreover, in contrast to the work of Mother Teresa, *philanthropy* entails mediation—it implies working through others who administer, design, serve, minister, or help. Although she may do more, the saint is down, dirty, and doing the job. Philanthropists may want to get involved (and I think that is no bad thing) but the distinctive task of philanthropy is enabling, providing resources. Philanthropists must work through others on the basis of a personal or institutional policy or plan.

Nonphilanthropic giving certainly requires work. Knowing what to give, when to give, and then finding the right gift requires energy, insight, imagination, and patience. I am regularly reminded of these facts because I am married to a mother of three and grandmother of five who spends countless hours of effort in trying (with great success) to identify appropriate gifts for birthdays and holidays. The fundamental problem really is not money; it is making the fact of love tangible. Indeed, diverting attention to money may lead the dedicated giver astray. Of course, not all persons are such careful and committed givers; I have been known to do considerable shopping in haste, with a much higher percentage of inappropriate or ill-chosen gifts. Tangible gifts are not the only, or perhaps the most important, things people give to each other, but they are not as trivial as some of us would like to pretend. They are sacramental tokens of love and friendship.

Philanthropic giving requires virtues much like those of the committed shopper. On the one hand it requires the ability to understand, listen, and learn. It calls for discernment. Without willingness to learn about the reality of the lives of recipients, many a well-intentioned gift will fall off-target. The patience that listening requires goes hand in hand with self-discipline. The hasty shopper lunges at the first attractive item in the store. The careful shopper does not. Impulse may have a part to play in this person's actions, but it is impulse schooled by experience and observation. Good philanthropic giving requires knowledge of the self and a commitment to a set of priorities. It is thought out and based in knowledge of the world into which the philanthropist hopes to enter.

Moreover, to be all that it should be philanthropy requires self-involvement. To be sure, objectives may be attained if the donor's self is kept completely in the background, but a price is paid for that—perhaps it would be better to say an opportunity is lost—for the donor. To take a terribly unflattering instance, Scrooge is helped by helping Bob Cratchit. The late New York philanthropist Brooke Astor was famous (infamous to some) for showing up among people in trouble wearing her best clothes and pearls. The criticism was that this was patronizing, but I think it might have been worse for Astor to have pretended to be something or someone she was not. And she was surely right, perhaps within her rights, to want to show up that way. The philanthropist who keeps too great a distance between herself and the actions done on her behalf protects herself from criticism and misunderstanding at a cost of learning, enjoying herself, and the chance to do better.

Why bother?

If anyone takes seriously what I have said so far, a natural response is to say that giving is morally ambiguous, diverts money from good uses in my own family, and takes a lot of time. Why do I bother with it? I have better things to do with my life. There are two powerful responses to this understandable point of view.

First, we need to involve ourselves in giving because we realize that we are part of something larger: a family, city, congregation, state, or nation. Or because we are among those persons dedicated to the cultural benefits of art and music, we are alumni of a college or professional school, or we are people who have been helped by a hospital. A surprising number give because they see themselves to have been befriended by a loving God. In any case we realize that *we are not alone, we are not unaffected by what happens to others.* We are a part of communities of memory and communities of shared hopes. Our lives are unintelligible apart from a distinctive series of social contexts and communities. For example, I am a suburban kid, a graduate of a midwestern college who then got professional training in the Ivies and has lived his life in the Midwest. I am a grandfather who is bolted to the pews of a university-town Episcopal church. My life is a synthesis of all these involvements, unintelligible apart from them except in fantasy. (I am somewhat disingenuously leaving out commitment to the support of various athletic teams.)

Thus we give in acknowledgment that we are not alone, not radically independent. We give from gratitude, we give to meet need, and we give because we are grateful for the chances we have had and the opportunities we see.

And we give philanthropically because we need help in adequately showing that gratitude. We have finite strength, vision, and time. With the scope of human need we have to work cooperatively, empowering others as best we can. We provide that help by example, by teaching, and by providing resources. What do we get out of it? An entirely legitimate sense of enjoying ourselves—maybe a whiff of transcendence and a kind of awareness that we have made a difference over the long haul.

In sum, we give to empower others in helping out and in doing so we fulfill ourselves. I have been very lucky to know and work with people who facilitate these activities and who are dedicated to helping meet human need and ministering to people trying to figure out what they can and should do.

Reference

Schervish, P. G., and Havens, J. J. "Millionaires and the Millennium: New Estimates of the Forthcoming Wealth Transfer and the Prospects for a Golden Age of Philanthropy" (unpublished paper). [www.bc.edu/research/swri/meta-elements/pdf/mrm.pdf]. Oct. 19, 1999.

DAVID H. SMITH *is Emeritus Professor of Religious Studies and director and Nelson Senior Scholar at the Poynter Center, Indiana University.*

Index

Back Issue/Subscription Order Form

Copy or detach and send to:

Jossey-Bass, A Wiley Imprint, 989 Market Street, San Francisco CA 94103-1741

Call or fax toll-free: Phone 888-378-2537; Fax 888-481-2665

Back Issues: Please send me the following issues at $29 each
                (Important: please include series initials and issue number, such as PF22)

_____

_____

$ _____   Total for single issues

$ _____   SHIPPING CHARGES: SURFACE   Domestic Canadian
                                   First Item $5.00 $6.00
                                   Each Add'l Item $3.00 $1.50
                Please call for next day, second day, or international shipping rates.

Subscriptions   Please ❏ start ❏ renew my subscription to _New Directions for Philanthropic Fundraising_ at the following rate:

U.S.	❏ Individual $109	❏ Institutional $215
Canada	❏ Individual $109	❏ Institutional $255
All Others	❏ Individual $133	❏ Institutional $289
Online Subscription		❏ Institutional $215

For more information about online subscriptions visit www.interscience.wiley.com

$ _____   Total single issues and subscriptions (Add appropriate sales tax for your state for single issue orders. No sales tax for U.S. subscriptions. Canadian residents, add GST for subscriptions and single issues.)

❏ Payment enclosed (U.S. check or money order only)

❏ VISA ❏ MC ❏ AmEx # _____ Exp. Date _____
Your credit card payment will be charged to John Wiley & Sons.

Signature _____ Day Phone _____

❏ Bill Me (U.S. institutional orders only. Purchase order required.)

Purchase order # _____
                 Federal Tax ID13559302   **GST 89102 8052**

Name _____

Address _____

_____

Phone _____ E-mail _____